AF413774

She Showed Up:

A Woman of Purpose, Power & Unstoppable Faith

Havana Book Group LLC.
Havanabookgrouppublishers.com

ISBN: 979-8-9927525-6-4

Published by
Havana Book Group LLC
Havanabookgrouppublishers.com

Table of Contents

Foreword

There are leaders—and then there are forces of nature. Lady Amb. Dr. Robbie Motter is the latter. As she approaches her 90th birthday, she is not slowing down; she is still rising, still building, still transforming the world—one life at a time. Her story is not just inspiring, it is a masterclass in courage, consistency, resilience, and the extraordinary power of showing up.

Lady Motter teaches us that life-changing impact begins with presence. She shows up for the unseen, the unheard, the overlooked. She shows up for women without mentors, for communities without hope, for young girls whose dreams have no platform. She shows up when it is uncomfortable, inconvenient, or seemingly impossible. And because she shows up, the world responds. Doors open. Opportunities appear. Lives transform.

Her mantra, "The power is in the asking," is not just advice—it is a revolution. She has asked boldly, acted decisively, and in doing so has built a global sisterhood of thousands of women, connecting hearts, minds, and dreams across continents. She does not simply lead; she lifts. She does not merely mentor; she ignites transformations that ripple through families, communities, nations, and generations.

Her work is global in scope and profoundly personal in impact. In Africa, Lady Motter has shown up in ways that redefine humanitarian service. She supported vulnerable communities through charity events, put her book in Kenya's national library, launched her work on the continent, and even had a tree planted in her name—a living, breathing symbol of the lives she touches and the hope she plants wherever she goes. These are not symbolic gestures; they are proof that a life devoted to service, empathy, and action can create tangible, enduring change.

GSFE—the Global Society for Female Entrepreneurs is a movement, a sanctuary, a global family where women are empowered to reach their fullest potential. Every connection Lady Motter cultivates, every mentorship she provides, every opportunity she opens, is a spark that lights fires of courage, purpose, and self-belief in women worldwide.

Lady Amb. Dr. Motter demonstrates that true leadership is not measured by crowns, awards, or accolades—it is measured by the lives you lift, the hope you give, and the courage you inspire. She has proven, time and again, that one person's persistence, heart, and vision can alter the trajectory of thousands of lives. She shows us that age is no limit to impact, that vision is timeless, and that courage can never be measured in years.

This book is not just her story, it is a call to action. It challenges every reader to rise with courage, to show up boldly even when it is difficult, to ask fearlessly even when the world says no, and to serve relentlessly even when it feels impossible. It is a blueprint for transformation. She proves that when you rise, you lift others. When you serve, you change worlds. When you lead with heart, humanity follows.

Lady Amb. Dr. Robbie Motter is a role model, a pillar of strength, a queen, and a beacon for every woman who has ever felt invisible or unheard. As you read these pages, let her story ignite something in you—the courage to show up, the audacity to ask, the commitment to serve, and the unwavering determination to transform not only your life but the lives of everyone you touch.

She has shown us what is possible. She has illuminated the path for generations. And now, it is our turn to rise. To lift. To lead. To serve. To create a world where no one walks alone, where kindness is currency, and where love, courage, and unity define our legacy.

Because this is more than a life, it is a movement. More than a story, it is a call. More than a book—it is an awakening. And Lady Amb. Dr. Robbie Motter is living proof that one life devoted to service, one heart committed to humanity, one woman willing to show up—can change the world.

Conclusion:
Let this book be your guide. Let her life be your inspiration. Show up. Ask boldly. Serve tirelessly. Lead with love. And in doing so, become the force of change that the world so desperately needs.

Powerful Quote to Close:
"Courage is not born from comfort; it is forged in the fire of showing up. Ask boldly, act fearlessly, and serve endlessly— and the world will rise with you."

By Professor Caroline Makaka
Founder & President, Leaders of All Nations International (LOANI)

Poem

Listen with your heart; let empathy lead the way,
Kindness can change the world in all we do and say.
Use your brain and God-given talents to create and to share,
Helping others rise, showing that you truly care.
Praise those who deserve it; let your genuine heart shine bright,
Love and support all people; bring warmth into the light.
No matter what race, color, sex, or belief they hold,
Nationality or faith—stand together, brave and bold.
Never judge another; keep your mind open and free,
For only with acceptance, can true harmony be.
We do not compete; we complete, as daughters and as sons,
We are One—united, till every battle's won.
Don't stay behind in the shadows when events call your name,
By showing up, you're living, and life's never quite the same.
Let go of hesitations; step forward without fear.
You'll find unexpected laughter, and warmth when friends are near.
And if you're feeling weary, don't let pride close the door,
Reach out and ask for guidance—it opens so much more.
A hand extended kindly, a smile that lights the night,
Will fill your soul with wonder and make all burdens light.
The joy that waits in places you almost didn't go,
Is proof that just by showing up, you help your spirit grow.
And when you dare to ask for help, instead of standing tall,
The answers and the caring may surprise and delight all.
So walk with open courage, and let your hope be seen,
Let wisdom guide your journey to places you've never been.

In giving and receiving, in laughter and in tears,
We build a world of kindness that outlasts all the years.
Together we create a future, hand in hand so true,
For love's the gentle promise that carries me and you.

This poem is a heartfelt call to embrace empathy and kindness in our daily lives. It encourages people to use their unique gifts to uplift others, to offer genuine praise and support, and to bring light into the world. The verses remind us that unity and acceptance—regardless of our differences in race, color, sex, nationality, or faith—are essential for true harmony. By keeping our minds open and refraining from judgment, we contribute to a society where we do not compete but rather complete and support one another. The closing line emphasizes the strength found in unity and the collective effort toward a world where everyone belongs.

A Poem on Empathy, Kindness, and Unity
Showing Up, Reaching Out, and the Joys They Bring

By Ambassador Dr. (h.c) Randi D. Ward
Ambassador Dr. (h.c) Randi Ward, 2020 IAOTP Educator of Decade/Top 50 Fearless Leaders; Co-Owner- RM Infinite; CEO Randi D. Ward, Author and Editor; Visionary Book Coach/14- time Best Seller Master Editor; 18-time International Best Seller, Author/Speaker; 2 Humanitarian Honorary Doctorate; LOANI Visionary Global Goodwill Ambassador; Humanitarian; 148 Multi-Award Recipient; International Student Mentor.

GSFE

CHAPTER 1 — The Girl Who Had No One

(But Became the Woman Who Helps Everyone)

Most people see the crown first.

They see the queen, the leader, the humanitarian, the connector of thousands of women, the CEO of a global nonprofit, and the woman who shows up everywhere — smiling, inspiring, organizing, lifting, and loving people into becoming the best version of themselves.

But what they don't know is that the woman who shows up so boldly today once lived in a world where no one showed up for her at all.

I was just fourteen when life pushed me into adulthood. No soft landing. No warm arms. No safety net. I was a young girl moving from foster home to foster home, trying to survive in a world far too big and far too cold for a child to face alone.

But even inside the loneliness, something was planted deep within me.

A whisper.

A promise.

A spark of purpose that said:

"Help others so no one ever feels like this."

That whisper became my compass.

It guided me through every challenge, every job, every reinvention, every hardship, and every opportunity. It shaped not only the woman I would become — but the mission that would define my entire life.

When you grow up without support, you learn two things very quickly:

How deep the hurt can go...
and how powerful kindness truly is.

Kindness became my fuel.
Connection became my calling.
Empowerment became my life's work.

I didn't have mentors — so I became one.
I didn't have a network — so I built one.
I didn't have someone to lift me — so I spent my life lifting thousands.

GSFE wasn't built from convenience.
It wasn't built because everything was easy.
It was built because a girl who needed help someday became a woman determined to ensure that no woman walks alone.

Every time I encourage a woman to dream bigger...

Every time I help someone break through fear...
Every time I say, "Show up and ask"
I am speaking to that younger version of myself, the girl who
needed someone to believe in her worth.

But here is the miracle:

That girl did more than survive.
She rose.
She built.
She led.
She became a global force for good.

I became the woman I needed as a child —
and that has become the legacy I give to the world

CHAPTER 2 — The Power of Showing Up

People often ask me,

"Robbie, what's your secret?
How did you build this incredible life, this global network, this legacy?"

I always smile, because the answer is so simple...
and yet it changes everything:

I showed up.

Not just when it was easy.
Not just when I felt strong.
Not just when I had the perfect outfit, the perfect words, or the perfect timing.

No — I showed up when I was tired, hurting, overwhelmed, unsure, or walking into a room where I didn't know a single soul.

And over the years, I discovered something magical:

Showing up is the hinge that swings open every door.

Every connection I've ever made...
Every opportunity that found me...

Every global relationship GSFE now holds...
Every award I've received...
Every woman who has transformed through our network...

Everything, absolutely everything, began with me showing up.
One moment, one room, one person at a time.

Showing Up Saved My Life

When I was young, I didn't have anyone showing up for me.
So, I made a promise, a promise to myself and to my future:

I would never miss a chance to show up, not for the world, and not for myself.

I walked into rooms where I felt invisible, and left with friends, collaborators, and lifelong connections.

I stepped into events where I felt out of place. and walked out with new dreams and an expanded vision.

I kept showing up, and eventually the world saw the woman I always knew I could be.

Showing up wasn't just a decision.
It became my power, and eventually, my purpose.

The Universe Answers Those Who Show Up

Some people call it luck.
Some call it coincidence.

But here's the truth:

Energy moves towards movement.
Blessings move towards action.
Opportunities move towards presence.

When you show up, the universe responds:

"She's ready.
Send her what she needs."

I've witnessed miracles unfold from the simple act of being in the right room.

A smile becomes a friendship.
A hello becomes a partnership.
A handshake becomes a global project.
A seat at the table becomes the start of a legacy.

And I've seen it again and again — not just in my life, but in the lives of the thousands I mentor.

The Miami Story: A Lesson in Divine Timing
Just this year, I flew to a conference in Miami, a room where I didn't know a single person and didn't speak the language. The entire event was in Spanish.

I could have stayed home.
I could have said, "This isn't for me."
I could have made excuses.
But that's not who I am.

And what happened?

They crowned me Queen of the Event.
I received an award.
I made powerful new friends.
And GSFE's Latino X network is now growing faster than ever.

Why?

Because I showed up.
And the room showed up for me.

Showing Up Is a Love Language
It tells people:

● You matter.
● I'm here.
● Your dreams deserve support.

When I walk into a GSFE meeting, I'm not just showing up physically.
I show up with my heart, my wisdom, my connections, my belief in every single person there.

This is why people follow me.
This is why people trust me.
This is why GSFE continues to rise on a global scale.

I don't just lead,
I show up for people, and they feel it.

Showing Up Creates Leaders

Everything I teach my women begins with this truth:

You can't grow if you don't show.
You can't win if you don't begin.
You can't receive it if you aren't in the room where the blessings live.
Your next connection...
Your next opportunity...
Your next breakthrough...
It's waiting for you.
But it cannot find you if you're hiding from the world.

My Message to You: Keep Showing Up

Even when you're uncomfortable.
Even when it's inconvenient.
Even when you're unsure.
Even when you're tired.
Even when you're afraid.

Show up anyway.

Your future self will thank you.
Your purpose will expand.
Your confidence will bloom.
Your blessings will multiply.
Your world will open in ways you cannot yet imagine.

Showing up changed my life,
and I promise you with all my heart:

It will change yours too.

CHAPTER 3 — A Lifetime of Lifting Women

If there is one thread woven through the entire fabric of my life, it is this:

I lift women.
I empower women.
I believe in women, often before they believe in themselves.
Not because it's trendy.
Not because it's easy.
Not because anyone expected it of me.
I do it because I know what it feels like to walk through the world without support...
and I vowed early in my life that no woman who crossed my path would ever feel alone.

It Started Nearly 50 Years Ago
Long before GSFE existed...
long before social media...
long before women had the visibility and platforms, they have today...
I was already helping them rise.

In the early days, I connected women to resources, jobs, opportunities, and—most importantly, to each other. This was before "networking" became a buzzword.
I lifted women through:

● Encouragement

- Tough love when needed
- Introductions
- Mentorship
- Wisdom
- Showing up (yes — even then)
- Genuine belief in their dreams

I didn't do it for recognition.
I didn't do it because someone taught me how.
I did it instinctively.
It was simply part of my soul's assignment.

NAFE: (National Association of Female Executives) The Foundation of a Movement

When I became the Global Coordinator of NAFE, I spent decades helping women across the country discover their voice, their power, and their confidence.
I created programs.
I built networks.
I trained leaders.
I spoke on many stages.
I mentored thousands.

I taught women how to:

- Think outside the box
- Ask boldly for what they wanted
- Believe opportunities always exist
- Understand that nothing is impossible
- Turn difficulties into learning moments
- Use positivity as a compass
- Stand tall, even in the storm

Those years built the foundation for the powerhouse I would later create.

Then Came GSFE: A Vision That Became a Global Sisterhood
In 2017, I didn't just start a nonprofit.
I lit a torch that ignited a movement.

GSFE was born from my heart, a home for women of every age, culture, and background. A safe, uplifting space for:

- Support
- Training
- Connection
- Opportunity
- Love
- Leadership
- A true sense of family

No one on our board is paid.
We serve from the heart, because service is who we are.

Today, GSFE has:

- Chapters across the country and around the world
- Directors who lead with integrity
- Collaborations with global humanitarian organizations
- Monthly meetings full of transformation
- Life-changing events
- Members joining from across the globe

But at its core, the heartbeat of GSFE remains beautifully simple:

Women lifting women.
Women empowering women.
Women believing in each other's dreams.

Why I Do It
Because I know what a woman becomes when someone believes in her.

She becomes brave.
She becomes bold.
She becomes unstoppable.
She becomes who she was always meant to be.

I've watched this metamorphosis thousands of times.
She walks in unsure.
She walks out shining.
She walks in doubting.
She walks out confident.
She walks in feeling small.
She walks out knowing she matters.

It is the most magical transformation in the world.

Stories I Will Never Forget
I've had women tell me:

● "Robbie, you changed my life."
● "You believed in me when no one else did."
● "You made me feel seen."

- "You helped me dream again."
- "I am who I am today because of GSFE."

Those words are the fuel of my heart.
Those stories are why I keep going.
They are the quiet miracles behind the movement.

In the testimony section of this book and others, you will hear stories from the very individuals being a member has helped, their stories matter and show how being a part of GSFE has changed their lives and opened doors even they never imagined.

The Ripple Effect

When you empower one woman, you don't just change her life.

You change her family.
You change her community.
You change her business, her impact, her future, and her legacy.

Empowered women empower others.
Loved women love stronger.
Encouraged women rise higher.
Connected women go further.

This is why my life's mission has always been, and will always be , lifting women.

The Truth Is... I Needed Them Too

People often think I'm the one doing all the giving.
But here is the secret:

Women have lifted me too.

Every smile.
Every hug.
Every thank you.
Every shared dream.
Every moment of trust.
Every story they've told me...

...has made me a better leader, a better woman, and a better soul.

This is not just my legacy.
This is our legacy, built together, heart to heart, hand in hand.

And the most beautiful part is this:

We are nowhere near finished.

CHAPTER 4 — Building
GLOBAL SOCIETY FOR FEMALE ENTREPRENEURS (GSFE):
A Movement, Not Just an Organization

GSFE didn't happen by accident.
It wasn't a casual idea or a spur-of-the-moment project.

GSFE was born from a lifetime of experience, compassion, resilience, and a deep knowing that women everywhere needed a community that felt like HOME.

A place where they could be seen.
A place where they could be supported.
A place where they could grow.
A place where they could lead.
A place where they could heal.
A place where they could win.

GSFE is not just an organization —
it is a movement, a sisterhood, a global family.

And building it has been one of the greatest callings of my life.

How It Started: A Vision Carried in My Heart
By 2017, after decades of leading, mentoring, and empowering women across the country, I felt something stirring inside me, a new mission, a deeper purpose.

I wanted to create something that brought together:

- Heart
- Leadership
- Mentorship
- Education
- Connection
- Service
- Community
- Global unity

Not just for entrepreneurs...
but for every woman with a dream.

GSFE was that dream.

I didn't want a program.
I didn't want a club.
I didn't want a membership service.

I wanted a place where women could truly THRIVE.
A network that made every woman feel:

- Valued
- Supported
- Encouraged
- Celebrated
- Safe
- Powerful
- And capable of more than she ever imagined

So, I created GSFE not from a business plan...

but from a heart wide open.

From One Spark to a Global Sisterhood
It began with one chapter...
then two...
then ten...
then twenty...

And today, GSFE has become a global force with:

● Directors who lead with integrity across states and countries
● Virtual networks connecting women worldwide
● Collaborations with international humanitarian
organizations
● A rapidly growing Latino X network
● A diverse community of authors, speakers, entertainers,
professionals, healers, and entrepreneurs

And the mission?
So simple, yet so powerful:

Empower. Inspire. Mentor. Educate. Connect.

Every meeting.
Every event.
Every message.
Every smile.

It all comes back to the mission.

GSFE is where women find their power, and their people.

The Secret: A Board That Serves From the Heart

The GSFE board is full of strong leaders...
but not even one of them is paid.

Not one.

Why?

Because GSFE is built on:

- Service, not profit
- Legacy, not ego
- Heart, not hierarchy

Every board member serves because they believe in the mission.
They believe in women.
They believe in what GSFE represents.

This is rare.
This is sacred.
This is why GSFE continues to grow with integrity, devotion,
and unstoppable love.

Events That Change Lives

Our events are not just gatherings —
They are experiences that reach the soul.

- Goddess celebrations
- International Women's Day Event
- International Kindness Day events
- Recognition ceremonies

- Book launches
- Charity drives
- Network meetings
- Retreats
- Trainings and workshops
- Humanitarian partnerships
- Global collaboration events
- Empowerment conferences

Women walk in curious...
and walk out transformed.

They feel connected.
They feel believed in.
They feel SEEN.

That is the true magic of GSFE.

The Collaborations That Lift Us Higher
GSFE continues to soar because of powerful alliances:

- LOANI (Leaders of All Nations International) Founded by
Dr, Caroline Makaka in London, England that is 139 countries,
- GIA (Global International Alliance) Founded and run by
Lady Amb. Lenora Wimberly Peterson Maclin
- International humanitarian leaders from all over the World.
- Authors, peace ambassadors, and global changemakers

These collaborations expand our reach, deepen our mission,
and unite us with people around the world who believe in
kindness, peace, and purpose-driven leadership.

The Culture of GSFE: We Don't Judge — We Lift

GSFE's culture is unlike anything else.

Here, women:
- Clap for each other
- Cheer for each other
- Celebrate each other
- Pray for each other
- Support each other
- Share opportunities
- Open doors
- And rise together

There is no competition.
There is no jealousy.
There is no "better than."

There is only this truth:

We rise by lifting others.

Why GSFE Is More Than an organization
Women don't just "join" GSFE...
they belong to it.

Inside GSFE, they find:

- Family
- Purpose
- Friendship
- Courage

- Leadership
- Momentum
- Healing
- Direction
- And a new version of themselves

GSFE is my heart's work.
My life's work.
My legacy.

It is the movement I will continue to build for as long as I
breathe.

Because a world where women are empowered
is a world where families thrive,
Communities rise,
and humanity heals.

And GSFE is helping build that world —
one woman at a time.

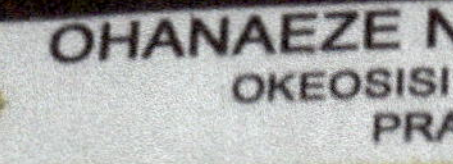

OHANAEZE NDIGBO KINGDOM
OKEOSISI II OF UGBAWKA
PRA EWUSI II

OHANAEZE KINGDOM
ROYAL PALACE OF OHANAEZE KINGDOM EZEIGBO CENTRAL REGION
GHANA
P.O.BOX A186 ADISADEL, CAPE COAST

HIS IMPERIAL MAJESTY KING OZOR DENNIS OKAFOR,
KING OF OHANAEZE KINGDOM
THIS IS TO CERTIFY THAT THE BEARER

HER MAJESTY QUEEN ROBBIE MOTTER

FROM CALIFORNIA USA, THE CEO OF GLOBAL SOCIETY FOR FEMALE ENTREPRENEURS
(GSFE)
HAS BEEN INSTALLED, INITIATED, CONFERRED WITH THE HONOR OF ROYAL TITLE OF:

QUEEN OF OHANAEZE KINGDOM IN CALIFORNIA USA

UNDER THE ANCESTRAL DECREE AND SEAL OF THE
OHANAEZE KINGDOM

THIS **16TH** DAY OF **MAY** 2024

HIS IMPERIAL MAJESTY KING DENNIS OZOR OKAFOR KING OF OHANAEZE KINGDOM,
OKEOSISI II OF UGBAWKA, PRA EWUSI II

President General
World Wide
H.I.M KING DENIS OZOR OKAFOR
OHANAEZE KINGDOM

CHAPTER 5 — Crowns, Confidence, and Courage

People often see me wearing a crown and assume it's just decoration, a glamorous touch, a fun accessory, or a nod to my many titles. And I truly am a Queen, my Queen title is: Her Majesty Queen Robbie Motter, Queen of OHANAEZE Kingdom in California received May 16, 2024. See certificate.

But if they only knew...

My crown is not about vanity.
My crown is not about royalty.
My crown is not about being "above" anyone.

My crown is a message, a symbol, and a mirror.

The Crown Is a Reminder
It reminds women to:

- stand tall
- reclaim their worth
- walk with dignity
- believe in their strength
- carry themselves like they matter
- show up like they belong

Because they DO.

A crown says:

"I am worthy.
I am enough.
I have purpose.
I am here."
And for many women, especially those who have been overlooked, unheard, dismissed, or silenced, that reminder can be life changing.

Why I Wear It

When I put on my crown, I'm not saying, "Look at me."
I'm saying:

"Look at what's possible."

I wear the crown for:

- The girl I used to be
- The woman I became
- The thousands of women I mentor
- The women still learning to believe in themselves
- The women who forgot their power
- The women still fighting to be heard

I wear it because it opens conversations.
I wear it because it inspires curiosity.
I wear it because it gives women permission to shine in their OWN way.

And let's be honest, a little sparkle never hurts anyone.

Confidence Is Earned, Not Given

People see my confidence now, but they often don't see the journey it took to build it.

Confidence didn't fall into my lap.

I built it.
I fought for it.
I grew it.
I claimed it.

It came from:

- Surviving what should have broken me
- Showing up when no one believed in me
- Walking into rooms alone and leaving with community
- Years of hard work, heartbreak, patience, and persistence
- Lifting others even when I was still learning to lift myself

My confidence is not loud or arrogant.
It is steady, grounded, earned, a quiet strength that speaks for itself.

Courage: The Quiet Force Behind Every Step

Courage doesn't always roar.
Sometimes courage whispers:

"Try again."
"Show up anyway."
"You can do this."

"Don't give up."
"Keep going."

Courage pushed me to:

- Build GSFE from the ground up
- Step onto global stages
- Collaborate with international humanitarian leaders
- Speak even when my voice shook
- Advocate for women who needed someone in their corner
- Continue giving and serving, even when life was heavy

Courage built my life.
And courage is what I teach every woman to carry with her. not as a shield, but as a compass.

Crowns Are Not Just for Queens, They Are for Every Woman

Every woman has a crown.

Some just forgot where they put it.
Some were told they weren't allowed to wear one.
Some were convinced they didn't deserve one.
And some never knew they had one in the first place.

I tell every woman:

"Your crown has been waiting for you. and it fits perfectly."

A crown is not about status; it is about self-worth.
A crown is not about perfection; it is about presence.

A crown is not about being better, it is about being brave.

When a woman sees herself as royalty, not in title, but in spirit, everything changes:

- Her posture
- Her confidence
- Her decisions
- Her voice
- Her purpose
- Her dreams

This is why I bring crowns to events.
This is why our Goddess theme is woven through GSFE.
Because I want women to FEEL majestic again.

I want them to remember the queen inside them.

A Crown Doesn't Make You a Queen, Your Heart Does

What truly makes a queen is:

- Her integrity
- Her kindness
- Her compassion
- Her generosity
- Her service
- Her leadership
- Her courage

- Her consistency
- her love

If there is one thing people know about me, it is this:

I lead with my heart first.
The crown simply reflects what's already there.

The Real Magic Behind the Crown

The greatest magic of the crown is what happens when other women see it.

Their eyes light up.
Their energy shifts.
Their confidence rises.
Their spirit awakens.
They begin to remember who they are.

And THAT —
that moment, that spark, that transformation —
is why I wear my crown.
Not to elevate myself...
but to elevate every woman who sees it.

CHAPTER 6 — Global Sisterhood & The Power of Unity

From the very beginning, I knew my mission was never meant to be small.
It was never meant to stay in one city, one state, or even one country.

My heart has always been global.

Because kindness is global.
Sisterhood is global.
Humanity is global.
Service is global.
And dreams?
Oh, dreams belong to the entire world.

Unity Is the Heartbeat of Everything I Do

GSFE didn't grow simply because women wanted business support.
It grew because women needed connection, belonging, and unity.

They wanted a place where:

- No one is left out
- No one is judged
- No one is forgotten

- No one is dismissed
- No one is alone

GSFE became that place —
a global home for women of every age, culture, background, and story.

Why Unity Matters

When women unite, they:

- Create change
- Heal communities
- Build businesses
- Raise leaders
- Support families
- Elevate nations

One woman is powerful.
But women together are unstoppable.

Unity isn't just a value I carry,
It is a responsibility.

A responsibility to bring women together.
A responsibility to break down walls.
A responsibility to bridge cultures.
It is a responsibility to create peace everywhere GSFE goes.

And that is exactly what we have done.

The Collaborations That Changed Everything

GSFE is strong,
but GSFE united with other global organizations became a force.

LOANI — Leaders of All Nations International

Led by Amb Dr. Caroline Makaka, LOANI is a true sister organization.
Together, we empower, honor, and uplift women around the world.
GSFE and LOANI stand side by side,
two movements, one heartbeat for humanity.

GIA — Global International Alliance

Led by Lady Amb Dr. Lenora Wimberly Peterson-Maclin, GIA opened doors for GSFE members to receive well-deserved honorary humanitarian doctorates. Over 100 of our members from our networks all over the world have received these honors in graduations in London, Paris, California, Las Vegas, Maryland and Texas and in 2026 we will do another graduation in Southern California.
These ceremonies are not just events.
They are acknowledgments of decades of service, compassion, and leadership.

These partnerships were not random.
They were divinely aligned.

When organizations serve with heart, integrity, and

compassion, unity becomes effortless.

Unity Across Cultures, Languages & Borders

One of the most beautiful things about GSFE is that it transcends every boundary.

I have stood in rooms where:

- People spoke different languages
- Wore different styles
- Came from different cultures
- Lived different lives

Yet, they felt like family instantly.

Why?

Because leadership, kindness, and humanity are universal languages.

This truth was never clearer than when I traveled to Miami for a conference conducted entirely in Spanish.

I didn't speak the language, but they spoke the language of heart.

And without a single translation, I was:

- Welcomed
- Embraced
- Celebrated

- Crowned
- Honored

That moment reminded me of something powerful:

When your heart is open, the world opens to you too.

The Global Ripple Effect

GSFE women are now:

- Serving communities
- Building nonprofits
- Leading humanitarian missions
- Writing books
- Hosting international events
- Mentoring others
- Speaking on global stages
- Empowering lives across continents

This is global sisterhood in action.

Every time a GSFE woman rises, the world rises with her.
Every time a woman finds her voice, she helps another woman find hers.
Every time we collaborate globally, we strengthen peace, unity, and human connection.

Why Unity Is My Legacy

I have always believed:
We are stronger together.

We are kinder together.
We are better together.

Unity isn't something I simply talk about —
it is something I LIVE.

It's why I show up consistently.
It's why I connect with people everywhere I go.
It's why I build bridges where others build walls.
It's why I partner with leaders who serve humanity with heart.
It's why I dedicate my life to empowering the world through women.

The world needs more unity.
And GSFE is helping build it,
one woman, one partnership, one act of kindness at a time.

The Soul of Our Movement

GSFE is more than a network.
It is more than a nonprofit.
It is more than a community.

GSFE is:

- A global sisterhood
- A circle of support
- A family without borders
- A community of leaders
- A movement of love, peace, and empowerment

And unity is the soul behind it all.

CHAPTER 7 — The Woman Behind the Awards

If someone followed me for just one month — maybe even one week — they would quickly notice something:

I give out a lot of awards.
A LOT.

Kindness Awards.
Goddess Awards.
Humanitarian Awards.
Legacy Awards.
Leadership Awards.
Peace Awards.
Certificates of Appreciation.
Recognition Honors.
Thank-you acknowledgments.

Some people ask me,
"Robbie, why do you give so many awards?"

My answer is simple:

Because people deserve to be seen.

The Power of Being Recognized

You never know what a person is carrying.
You never know what battles they're fighting, or what storm they're walking through.
Sometimes a woman is holding herself together with nothing but faith, hope, and sheer willpower.

And then... she hears her name.

She walks across a room.
She receives an award — sometimes the very first award of her entire life.
She feels her heart lift, her confidence rise, and her spirit return to life.

That moment changes her.

I LIVE for those moments.

Because recognition isn't about ego —
it's about worth. It's about being seen. It's about being valued.

My Purpose in Giving Awards

I give awards to:

● Honor service
● Celebrate kindness
● Acknowledge courage

- Reward leadership
- Uplift humanitarian work
- Shine a light on the overlooked
- Remind people their goodness matters
- Strengthen purpose
- Restore hope
- And — most of all — to make people feel valued

Awards are not just plaques or paper.
They are emotional lifelines.
They are permission slips to keep going.
They are proof that someone's efforts have meaning.

The Goddess Awards: Celebrating the Divine Feminine

One of my most cherished traditions is honoring women as Goddesses.

Why Goddesses?

Because every woman carries:

- Beauty
- Strength
- Intuition
- Resilience
- Creativity
- Leadership
- And her own magic

Whether she fully believes it yet or not.

When a woman receives a Goddess Award, something shifts inside her.
She begins to see herself differently.
She remembers who she truly is.
She realizes she is powerful, worthy, and capable.

And often... she goes home and does something extraordinary.

Kindness Day: Where Hearts Become Visible

International Kindness Day is one of my favorite celebrations — not because of the crowns or the glamor, but because kindness is the language of the soul.

On that day:

- Every guest shines
- Every entertainer is honored
- Every volunteer is appreciated
- Every helper is acknowledged
- Every vendor is celebrated
- Every award feels like a hug
- Every smile lights the room

People leave feeling:

- Loved
- Valued
- Uplifted
- Appreciated

And that is the real award.

Humanitarian Recognitions: Honoring Those Who Serve Humanity

Through my collaboration with global humanitarian leaders — especially Lady Amb Dr. Lenora Wimberly Peterson-Maclin of GIA — I have witnessed countless men and women receive honorary humanitarian doctorates.

These ceremonies are spiritual.

As I stand on the stage, watching each recipient receive their sash, medallion, and degree, I think:

"This is what humanity looks like."

Service.
Compassion.
Dedication.
Love.
Leadership.
Integrity.
Heart.

These honors elevate GSFE, uplift the mission, and celebrate the lifetime service of our women and men around the world.

What People Don't See

People see:

- The sparkle
- The crowns
- The beautiful certificates
- The awards on the tables
- The elegance, the gowns, the photos

But they don't see:

- The hours I spend writing every word
- The careful thought behind each award
- The late nights preparing
- The phone calls and messages
- The logistics
- The prayerfully chosen names
- The love poured into every detail

Every award is intentional.
Every award carries meaning.
Every award says:

"I see you.
I value you.
You matter."

Why I Do It — The Real Reason

Because I remember being the girl no one celebrated.

The girl no one believed in.
The girl who grew up without applause, without recognition, without acknowledgment.
The girl who never heard her name called for something good.

I vowed that if I ever had the power to honor others...
I would do it every chance I could.

Because a single acknowledgment can change someone's life.
It can awaken purpose.
It can restore hope.
It can heal wounds.
It can ignite new beginnings.

The Woman Behind the Awards

Who am I behind the scenes?

A woman who loves people deeply.
A woman who sees the good in everyone.
A woman who celebrates every victory — big or small.
A woman who believes no act of kindness should go unnoticed.
A woman who knows recognition is one of the purest forms of leadership.
A woman who's joy is watching others shine.
A woman who gives because giving is her nature.

A woman who shines the light on others, even while standing
in her own.

And yes —
a woman who will hand out a crown or certificate any chance
she gets...

because she knows exactly how powerful one moment of being
seen truly is.

CHAPTER 8 — The Heart of a Humanitarian Queen

Some people collect titles.
Some collect achievements.
Some collect applause.

But me?

I collect people.
I collect stories.
I collect moments of kindness and opportunities to help.
I collect lives I can make just a little better.

That is what makes my heartbeat.
That is what makes me a humanitarian, long before the world ever called me one.

Humanitarian Isn't What I Do — It's Who I Am

From a very young age, I understood what pain felt like.
I understood what loneliness felt like I understood what struggling felt like.

So, I made a promise to myself:

If I can help someone, I will.
If I can lift someone, I must.

And I have lived that promise every single day of my life.

Helping others isn't something I schedule.
It isn't a task on a to-do list.
It isn't an event.

It is the air I breathe.

Service: My Lifelong Purpose

People see me on stages.
They see the crowns, the awards, the elegance, the photos, and the events.

But my real work happens quietly... softly... daily...
and often without a single witness.

It happens when:

- I answer a late-night call from someone in tears
- I text encouragement at 2:00 a.m.
- I connect someone to a job, a resource, or a new beginning
- I speak life into a woman who thinks she is broken
- I lift someone who believes they have nothing left
- I mentor someone who feels lost and forgotten
- I show up for someone who just needs hope
- I write my weekly positive message to all to life their spirits
and to let them know anything is possible.

Humanitarian work is not about big gestures.
It is about consistent love.
Steady compassion.
Everyday kindness.

The Crown and the Queen

People call me Queen Robbie, and yes, the crown sits beautifully.

But my true royalty comes from:

- My heart
- My compassion
- My loyalty
- My 50+ years of service
- My dedication to humanity
- My belief in every person's worth
- My refusal to give up on people

Leadership is not about standing above others.
It is about standing with them and sometimes holding them up until they can stand again.

GSFE: My Global Humanitarian Mission

GSFE is more than a network, it is a humanitarian movement.

We lift:

- Women in crisis
- Women starting over

- Women building businesses
- Women healing from loss
- Women rebuilding their confidence
- Women who feel unseen
- Women ready to rise

We support each other through:

- Illness
- Grief
- Financial hardship
- Emotional stress
- Life transitions
- Dreams being born and reborn

GSFE is a lighthouse for women, and I am honored to guide that light.

Humanitarian Partnerships: Expanding the Heartbeat

My work with global humanitarian organizations has given me the gift of lifting even more lives.

LOANI — Leaders of All Nations International

With Amb Dr. Caroline Makaka, LOANI honors kindness, peace, and global service. Together, we uplift women on an international scale.

GIA — Global International Alliance

Under Lady Amb Dr. Lenora Wimberly Peterson-Maclin, GIA recognizes humanitarian leaders with honorary doctorate degrees — powerful acknowledgments of a life devoted to serving others.

These partnerships weren't accidental.
They were divinely aligned. born from shared values, shared hearts, and shared devotion to humanity.

What is amazing that we three are all a nonprofit and in 2026 will celebrate ten years of serving.

The Soft Strength Behind My Smile

People see my smile and think my life has been easy.

But my smile was built in storms.
My compassion came from struggle.
My strength came from survival.
My kindness came from knowing what it felt like to have none.
My leadership came from a childhood of standing alone and deciding that no one else should ever feel that way.

- I serve because I know what it is to need help.
- I lead because I know what it is to be lost.
- I give because I know what it is to have nothing and still rise.

My heart was shaped in the hard places —
and that is what makes it so strong.

The Humanitarian Queen's Philosophy

My philosophy is simple:

Be the person you needed when you were young.
Be the one who shows up.
Be the one who cares.
Be the one who believes in people.
Be the one who lifts the broken.
Be the one who sees the invisible.
Be the one who leads with love.
Be the one who chooses kindness every single time.

Kindness is not weakness.
It is the greatest strength in the world.

Why I Will Never Stop

At 89, and soon to be 90 on March 8, 2026 International
Women;s Day, most people slow down.
Not me.
My purpose still burns bright.
My mission still calls me.
My service is still needed.
My heart still has work to do.

As long as I can speak,
as long as I can move,
as long as I can send a message,
as long as I can show up...

I will continue lifting humanity, one person at a time.

Because this is not just my calling —
it is my legacy.

I am not just a humanitarian.
I am a woman who LOVES people.

And that love —
that unstoppable, unwavering, unconditional love —

That is what makes me a queen.

CHAPTER 9 — Books, Authors, and Stories That Change the World

Some people write books.
But me?
I ignite them.
For years, I've believed that every woman carries a story inside her — a story that can heal, empower, inspire, and transform lives.
But many women never get the chance to share it.
They think:

"Who would want to hear my story?"

- "I'm not a writer."
- "I don't know where to start."
- "My life isn't special enough."

Oh, but it is.
Every life is extraordinary.
Every story matters.
Every journey has purpose.
And that is why I began creating anthologies.
Not to sell books —
but to change lives.
The lives of the writers... AND the readers.

The Birth of a Global Storytelling Movement

GSFE was never just about empowering women entrepreneurs.
It was about helping women find — and OWN — their voice.
One day, a thought came to me so clearly it felt like it had been
waiting for years:
What if I brought women together from around the world to
tell their stories...
and treated each story like the masterpiece it is?
So I did.
I created books that became platforms.
Platforms that became movements.
Movements that became global waves of empowerment.
These books didn't just share stories.
They awakened women.

The Anthologies That Made History

Over the years, I've guided women into writing powerful,
transformative books such as:
What Is Your WHY? Unlock Your Desired Life by Finding
Clarity
Voices of Peace — which became an international bestseller
and is now placed in the historic Alexandria Library
Catalyst for Change
One World, One Heart
Legacy of Courage
The Power Within
 Passion-Driven Leadership
Purpose in My Pulse
And so many more...
Each book became a home for dozens — sometimes hundreds
— of voices.
Women who had never written before suddenly became

authors.
Women who thought their pain didn't matter realized it did.
Women who doubted their worth stepped fully into their power.
These books didn't just make bestsellers —
they made believers.

Why I Love Anthologies

Anthologies are magic because they give women:
 A voice
 A platform
 A sisterhood
 A legacy
They teach women:
how to put their heart on paper
 How to tell their truth
 How to turn wounds into wisdom
 How to transform testimony into triumph
 How to inspire someone they may never meet
 When that book is finally published, each woman looks at her chapter and whispers:
"I DID that. I am an author."

That transformation is priceless.

Books That Build Community, Not Competition

In my anthologies, no one competes.
Every woman shines.
Every story is sacred.
Instead of comparison, there is collaboration.

Instead of ego, there is encouragement.
Instead of judgment, there is joy.
Instead of fear, there is freedom.
This is why the books succeed again and again —
they are created with love, not pressure.

Launches That Feel Like Royal Celebrations

My book launches are not simple signings —
They are EXPERIENCES.
There are:
Ceremonies
Certificates
 Awards
Photoshoots
 Crowns
 Music
 Speeches
Hugs
 Tears
Smiles
Global recognition
Every co-author is honored like royalty.
Every story is treated like treasure.
Every woman feels like she belongs on that stage.
Book launches are my way of saying:
"Your voice matters.
Your life matters.
Your contribution matters."

Stories That Travel the World

My books have crossed oceans.
They've reached Africa, Europe, Asia, the Caribbean, South America, and beyond.
Authors have traveled internationally to sign them.
Libraries have requested them.
Conferences have highlighted them.
Readers have cried over them.
And every time a book ships to a new place, it carries something powerful:
the heart of a woman who dared to share.

The Ripple Effect: Healing Beyond the Pages

When a woman writes her story, she doesn't just heal herself —
she heals someone else too.
I've received messages like:
"This chapter saved me."
"I felt like she was telling my story."
I finally feel seen."
 "This book gave me hope."
That is the true victory.
That is why I keep creating more books.
That is why I invest my time, my energy, and my heart into every project.
Because stories are lifelines.
Stories are medicine.
Stories are bridges.

Why I Will Always Believe in Stories

- Stories build connection.
- Stories build confidence.
- Stories build community.
- Stories change families.
- Stories transform futures.
- Stories unite strangers.
- Stories heal the world.

I build anthologies because I believe in women.
And I believe in the power of their truth.
My mission is simple:
Help women tell their stories,
so they can change their world —
and eventually, the world.
And we are just getting started.

CHAPTER 10 — Legacy: Creating Leader Who Will Continue the Mission

Legacy isn't about what you leave behind.
Legacy is about what you leave within people.

I have spent my entire life pouring into others, lifting them, teaching them, believing in them, and preparing them for more than they ever imagined they could become.

Because I never wanted GSFE to be a moment
I wanted it to be a movement.
A movement that would continue long after I'm gone — carried by the hearts, hands, and leadership of every woman I've ever poured into.

Leadership With a Heart , The Robbie Way

Leadership isn't about titles, positions, or recognition.

Leadership is:

- Showing up
- Giving your best
- Serving without expectation
- Lifting those around you
- Mentoring the next generation
- Planting seeds you may never live to see bloom

This is the leadership I teach.

This is the leadership I model.

Not from the top,
but from the center, where people feel seen, safe, believed in,
and respected.

True leadership doesn't demand attention.
It inspires it.

Building Leaders, One Woman at a Time

Over the years, I've watched women who once whispered, " grow into women who now ROAR".

I've watched women who:

- Doubted themselves; become directors
- Felt invisible, doubted themselves, become speakers
- Thought they were ordinary, become extraordinary
- Had lost their spark find it again
- Were afraid to lead blossom into powerful mentors
- Believed they were alone find a global family

GSFE doesn't just develop entrepreneurs.
GSFE develops leaders, heart leaders, servant leaders, world changers.

My Directors: The Daughters of My Legacy

Every GSFE director holds a chapter of my heart.

They lead with:

- Integrity
- Compassion
- Consistency
- Faith
- Love
- Strength
- And fierce dedication

They carry the mission forward in different cities, different states, and different countries, yet always with the same passion that began in my living room many years ago.

They are:

- Teachers
- Healers
- Speakers
- Authors
- Mentors
- Mothers
- Sisters
- Queens
- Community Warriors

These are the women who will keep GSFE alive for generations.

The Mission Must Outlive the Founder

I have always been clear about my purpose:

GSFE will continue long after me.

Not because of documents, websites, or systems,
but because of the leaders I've raised.

Women who have watched me:

- Lead
- Serve
- Love
- Give
- Honor others
- Build community
- Show up
- Rise after storms
- Stay positive in adversity
- And never stop believing

Women who know how to wear a crown with humility and
responsibility.
Women who understand that leadership isn't about spotlight,
it's about service.

Preparing for the Next Generations

My legacy is not just for today's women.
It is for:

- Their daughters
- Their granddaughters
- The young women watching from the sidelines
- The girls growing up needing someone to believe in them

I want future generations to know:

- Kindness wins
- Service matters
- Unity heals
- Women can lead
- Dreams are worth chasing
- Strength is built, not given
- Leadership begins with love

GSFE was built for them too —
even if they don't know it yet.

A Future Filled with Purpose

The next era of GSFE will be global in ways we only dreamed of:

- More international chapters
- More anthologies
- More humanitarian missions
- More peace initiatives
- More collaborations
- More global partnerships
- More empowered leaders
- More lives transformed

And when those future directors tell their stories, I hope they begin them with:

"A woman named Robbie believed in me, and because of her, I believed in myself."

My True Legacy

My legacy is not the crown on my head.
My legacy is the crowns I place in the hands of others.

My legacy is not GSFE as an organization.
My legacy is the sisterhood it created.

My legacy is not the awards I received.
My legacy is the awards I gave.

My legacy is not counted in years,
it is counted in impact.

My legacy is every woman I encouraged,
every woman I lifted,
every woman I inspired,
every woman I trained,
every woman I believed in,
every woman who found her voice because I found mine.

The Baton Is Already in Motion

I have already passed pieces of my mission to so many extraordinary souls.

They carry it with:

- Pride
- Honor
- Gratitude
- Devotion
- And deep love for the work of what I created.

And when the day comes that I can no longer lead with my feet,
I will still lead with my heart and legacy.

CHAPTER 11 – What They Don't Know About Robbie

Most people know the women before "the crown".
They know the CEO.
They know the connector.
They know the humanitarian.
They know the one who shows up everywhere, lifting everyone around her.

But there is another Robbie, the woman behind the sparkle, that many never see.

And she is just as important as the leader the world watches.

They Don't Know How Soft My Heart Really Is

People see my strength first.
They see my confidence, my leadership, my drive.

But what they often don't see is my softness...

- How deeply I love
- How quickly I forgive
- How naturally I nurture
- How easily I cry when someone is hurting
- How my heart aches for people I barely know
- How I feel every story people share with me

My strength is what people admire...

but my softness is where my heart lives.

They Don't Know How Much I Worry About Others

Behind the scenes, I think about people constantly.

I wonder:

- "Is she okay?"
- "Does he have what he needs?"
- "Does she know someone cares?"
- "Who needs encouragement today?"
- "Who needs a message or a text to show how much I care?"

People don't know how many nights I stay awake thinking about someone else's struggle.

That is just who I am.

They Don't Know How Many Times I've Pushed Through Pain

If people knew the physical, emotional, and spiritual pain I've gone through,
and STILL showed up
they would understand that courage isn't loud.

I've walked into events:

- Tired
- Hurting
- Grieving

- Overwhelmed
- Carrying heavy responsibilities

with a heart full of things no one else knew

And still, I smiled.
I showed up.
I lifted others.

Not because it was easy...
but because helping people gives me strength.

They Don't Know How Much I Do Quietly

Most of what I do never gets posted or announced.

People don't see:

- The groceries I've bought
- The calls I've answered, in late hours
- The bills I've helped with
- The rides I've given
- The opportunities I've created
- The people I've encouraged when no one knew

A lot of my kindness is silent, but it is real.
And it comes straight from my heart.

They Don't Know How Funny I Really Am

People see the leader...
But they don't always see the woman who loves to joke, laugh,

tease, and sparkle up a room.

I'm not serious all the time.
I love fun.
I love to make people smile.
And I can light up a room with laughter just as quickly as I can
with wisdom.

They Don't Know How Strong My Faith Is,

My strength doesn't come from crowns, titles, or events.

It comes from my faith.
From the quiet conversations I have with God.
From trusting His timing.
From believing every hardship shaped me for a reason.

My faith keeps me grounded and keeps my heart open.

They Don't Know How Often I Put Myself Last

I will skip meals... skip rest... skip breaks...
all because someone needs me.

That is my heart.
That is my nature.

I don't do it for recognition.
I do it because I care deeply.

People follow me not because I'm perfect...
but because I love fully.

They Don't Know How Much I've Overcome

If people knew the storms I've survived...

the heartbreaks,
the losses,
the betrayals,
the challenges,
the mountains...
And STILL I rise...

They would understand why I fight so hard for others.

I didn't become strong because life was easy.
I became strong because I refused to give up.

They Don't Know How Much Love I Carry

I love deeply.
I love quickly.
I love wholeheartedly.

My heart is big enough to hold the world —
and that is something few people truly see.

What They Don't Know... Is What Makes Me Who I Am

Behind the woman is:

- A survivor
- A giver

- A warrior
- A mentor
- A mother, sister, friend, guide
- A woman who keeps loving
- A heart that keeps caring
- A soul that keeps rising

What they don't know about me...
is exactly what makes me who I am.

And it's why the world shines a little brighter wherever I go.

Because GSFE is not just my organization —
it is my life's purpose living in the hearts of thousands.

My legacy is safe.
My legacy is strong.
My legacy is alive now and forever.

I have created leaders, and leaders build the future.

CHAPTER 12 — The Woman Who Never Stops Giving

If there is one thing the world can say about me without hesitation, it is this:

I give.
I give.
And then, I give some more.

Not because I have everything —
but because I know what it feels like to have nothing.

Not because life has always been easy,
but because I learned early that kindness is the only real wealth we take with us.

Not because I expect anything in return,
but because giving is my joy, my purpose, my service, and my heartbeat.

Giving Is My First Language

Some people speak with words.
I speak with actions.

My giving shows up in:

- A text sent at just the right moment
- A message that lifts a hurting soul
- A crown placed on someone who forgot her worth
- A call to check on someone
- A connection that changes a life
- An award that restores confidence
- A meal, a hug, a smile
- Showing up when I'm tired, busy, or hurting
- Creating opportunities for others to shine

I give because I see people.
I give because I care.
I give because giving is who I am.

Giving Is the Way I Love

When I love someone, I pour into them.

I pour:

- Encouragement
- Support
- Energy
- Belief
- Guidance
- Wisdom
- Kindness
- Time
- Connection

I love loudly.
I love boldly.
I love completely.

I don't love in halves,
I love in full.

Giving Even When No One Knows

Most of what I give never becomes public.

People never see:

- The financial help
- The groceries dropped off quietly
- The private messages to someone in crisis
- The prayers whispered in silence
- The doors opened for someone struggling
- The opportunities created for someone afraid to ask
- The comfort given to someone grieving
- The advocacy done behind the scenes

I am not a spotlight giver.
I am a heart giver.

Giving When I'm Hurting Too

People often think I give because I'm always strong.

But the truth is...

I give even when I am:

- Tired
- Overwhelmed
- In pain
- Carrying my own burdens
- Recovering from loss
- Facing challenges no one knows about

Giving heals me.
Giving fuels me.
Giving reminds me of my purpose.

When I help someone else rise, I rise a little higher too.

Why I Never Stop

I don't give to be thanked.
I don't give to be honored.
I don't give for applause.
I don't give for attention.

I give because:

- People need someone
- People need hope
- People need encouragement
- People need compassion
- People need a second chance
- People need community
- People need love

And I know exactly what it feels like to need all those things.

GSFE: A Legacy of Giving

GSFE is not just a network —
it is a giving machine.

Every meeting, every event, every connection carries the spirit
of generosity.

We give:

- Opportunities
- Platforms
- Support
- Mentorship
- Recognition
- Love

Generosity is the DNA of GSFE because it is the DNA of its
founder.

Giving Has Given Me More Than I Ever Expected

The world says I give endlessly, and I do.

But life has also given back to me:

- Friendships
- Miracles

- Blessings
- Love
- Community
- Respect
- Purpose
- Joy
- A global family

The more love I give,
the more love returns to me in beautiful ways.

Giving Is My Forever Legacy

I may not have material riches,
but I am rich in what truly matters:

- Love
- Faith
- Kindness
- Service
- Compassion
- People
- Purpose

I want people to remember me not just as a leader —
but as a giver.

Someone who:

- Showed up
- Reached out

- Stepped in
- Lifted others
- Helped wherever she could
- Made life softer
- Made the world kinder

I want my life to be a message —
a reminder that kindness is never wasted, and giving is the greatest gift we leave behind.

The Woman Who Never Stops Giving, Still Has More to Give

Even now, at 89 years old, I am still planning events, mentoring, connecting, organizing, lifting, and dreaming.

And on International Women's Day, March 8th, 2026, I will proudly celebrate turning 90 years old, still giving, still serving, still loving, still showing up.

Because as long as I am alive,
my purpose is alive too.

Giving is not something I do,
it is who I am.

And I will keep giving,
loving,
serving,
and showing up
until my very last breath.

CHAPTER 13 — Your Crown, Your Purpose, Your Future

If there is one thing life has taught me, it is this:

Purpose never retires.
Purpose never fades.
Purpose grows as long as you grow.

And my purpose, to empower, uplift, mentor, inspire, and connect, is still burning bright.
The crown I wear is not just a symbol of who I became...
it is a promise of who I am still becoming.

The Crown I Wear Is the Crown I Earned

There was a time in my life when I owned nothing.
No safety.
No support.
No certainty.
No family cheering me on.
No one showed up for me.

But I always had purpose, even before I knew its name.

And with every challenge, every act of service, every woman I helped, every meeting I led, every hand I held, every event I organized...

I earned my crown.

Not from royalty.
Not from privilege.
But from resilience, love, and service.

My crown is made of:

- Compassion
- Courage
- Survival
- Leadership
- Kindness
- Integrity
- An unshakeable love for people

This is why it shines.
This is why it fits.
This is why women see it and feel stronger.

My Purpose Was Written in My Heart Long Ago

My purpose began the moment I understood that if I didn't help myself, no one else would.

And as the years went on, that purpose grew into something bigger:

If I could survive without help...
Then I would become the help others needed.

My purpose is to:

- Lift
- Mentor
- Encourage
- Connect
- Create opportunity
- Give hope
- Build community
- Honor humanity
- Build leaders
- And always, always, show up

That purpose has led me through decades of service, and it guides me every single day.

My Future Is Still Unfolding, And It's Big

At 89 years old, and almost 90, people expect me to slow down.
But the truth is…
I'm just beginning the next chapter of my mission.

My future still includes:

- Launching more anthologies
- Training new directors
- Expanding GSFE globally
- Building more humanitarian partnerships
- Hosting kindness, peace, and unity events
- Honoring more women
- Writing more books
- Creating opportunities for people to shine

- Connecting nations
- And continuing to show up wherever God sends me

The year 2026 will be powerful,
GSFE's 10-year anniversary,
and on International Women's Day, March 8, I will proudly
celebrate turning 90 years old.

My future isn't slowing down —
it's rising.

MY Mission Is Far from Done

I still have:

- People to touch
- Leaders to mentor
- Events to host
- Stories to preserve
- Books to write
- Crowns to place
- Kindness to spread
- Networks to build
- And lives to change

The mission continues because I continue.

The World Still Needs My Light

I've built a global sisterhood.
I've empowered thousands.
I've mentored leaders on multiple continents.

I've lifted humanity through kindness, unity, and service.

But the truth is,
The world still needs Robbie.

It needs:

- My wisdom
- My compassion
- My leadership
- My belief in people
- My ability to connect strangers into family
- My way of lifting people when they forget their worth

My voice still has more to teach.
My heart still has more to give.
My crown still has more to lead.

My Future Legacy: A World I Helped Heal

Long after I'm gone, the world will still feel my presence through:

- Every director I raised
- Every author I empowered
- Every certificate I gave
- Every act of kindness I inspired
- Every collaboration I built
- Every ripple of love that began with me

My legacy is not a chapter.

It is an entire library.

A living archive of service, love, courage, and compassion.

The Final Truth

My crown is not heavy,
because it was forged from purpose, not pride.

My purpose is not finished,
because my heart still has work to do.

My future is not fading,
because my light grows brighter with every life I touch.

I am not done.
I am not slowing.
I am not stepping back.

I am stepping into the most powerful, meaningful, and legacy-building chapter of my life.

And the world, my GSFE family, my LOANI family, my GIA family, and my thousands of sisters and brothers, will continue walking with me, rising with me, and shining with me.

My crown is steady.
My purpose is alive.
My future is radiant.

This is not the end.
This is the beginning of my greatest impact yet.

Dedication

This book is dedicated to every soul who believed in me, walked beside me, or whispered encouragement when I needed it most.

To my children Ed, Lisa, Lori, grandchildren, Heather, Joe, Jessica, Amber, and great-granddaughter, Rory, you are the roots of my strength and the reason I keep showing up with purpose and love. They have taught me what love, sacrifice, and diligently serving really means and matters.

Family means so much to me and always has. It has been my driving force.

To my GSFE and LOANI sisters and brothers around the world, your courage, your brilliance, and your unwavering hearts inspire me every single day.

And to every person I have met, and all those I've yet to meet, thank you for the light you bring to this world.

You are all a part of my story and life, and I am grateful for you.

About Lady Amb Dr. h.c. Robbie Motter

Lady Ambassador Dr.(h.c.) Robbie Motter is the Founder & CEO of the Global Society for Female Entrepreneurs (GSFE), a 501(c)(3) nonprofit that empowers, mentors, educates, and connects women, and now men and youth around the world. With over 50 years of service and leadership, she has dedicated her life to uplifting others, showing them the power of showing up, asking, believing in themselves, and turning challenges into stepping-stones.

Robbie's journey began with hardship, on her own at 14, moving through foster homes, learning to survive and thrive without guidance. Yet she turned her pain into purpose, becoming a lifelong mentor and catalyst for change.

Known as "The Connector," Robbie has helped thousands of individuals grow their businesses, discover their gifts, and rise into their greatness. She has received hundreds of awards for her humanitarian service and global impact, and her collaborations with organizations like LOANI (Leaders of All Nations International) and GIA (Global International Alliance) that have changed lives worldwide.

At 89 — soon to be 90 on International Women's Day, March 8, 2026, she continues to serve daily with energy, passion, and grace. Robbie believes purpose never stops, and she remains committed to inspiring future generations through leadership, service, and love.

Acknowledgments

My journey has been blessed with extraordinary people, and I honor you here with all my heart.

To my beloved children Ed, Lori, Lisa, grandchildren, Heather, Joe, Jessica, Amber, and great-great granddaughter Rory, You have been my joy, my purpose, and my greatest inspiration. Every success and every chapter of my life carry a piece of you in it and with it.

To my treasured GSFE sisters and brothers, thank you for believing in a vision bigger than all of us and for showing up with your gifts, your love, and your courage. Together, we empower the world.

To Dr. Caroline Makaka the founder/Ceo of LOANI and all my beautiful global LOANI family, thank you for your kindness, unity, and strength. Your hearts shine so brightly and for presenting me with the beautiful Lady title you honored me with in London many years ago on my first trip to London...

To Lady Amb. Dr. Lenora Wimberly Peterson Maclin, thank you for all the great opportunities you have offered our GSFE members to be honored with their Honorary Humanitarian Doctorate degrees.

To Queen Eden S Trinidad, thank you for your kindness to all our GSFE members and the beautiful awards you have sent to GSFE over the years, also a heartfelt thank you for recommending me to the King to receive my official Queen title.

Also, to the countless GSFE sisters that I love and to so many friends I have met, and the many I will meet in the days to come, thank you for walking with me, inspiring me, and allowing me to pour love and purpose into your lives.

You are all part of my legacy

I also love the Legacy that all the GSFE books will leave of the books we have written with the help of our great members and our fabulous publisher Amb. Dr. Angela Covany, owner of Havana Book Group Publishers and the wonderful talents of Amb Dr. Marcy Decato, a co-partner with Creative Solutions Marketing Riverside, Ca. who does the layout for all our books.

We are honored that all our books made US and International #1 best sellers on day of launch in numerous categories and platforms and inspired some to write books of their own.

These books all share beautiful stories all over the world. They inspire, impact lives, and share insightful stories of resilience and strength. The books, all are in the oldest library in the world before Christ in Alexandria, Egypt thanks to GSFE sister Dr, Randi Ward who made that connection for us.

Out latest book vol 4 of Its "All About Showing Up and the Power is in the Asking" will be published in 2026 and launched on the Leaders of All Nations LOANI) trip to Nepal and India in October 2026 that GSFE members are also invited to attend.

All these books are available on Amazon US and UK and other Amazons across the globe, Barnes n Noble, and bookstores US and International. Our 2025 book What is Your Why" is in libraries in Kenya, Africa.

Testimonies

"These are not endorsements. They are reflections. They are voices of lives touched, lifted, and changed, not by perfection but by presence."

A Testimony of Eternal Gratitude to Dr. Robbie Motter. How She Blessed, Lifted, and Forever Rewrote the Destiny of a Queen and an Entire Nation.

There are angels who walk this earth in human form. Dr. Robbie Motter is chief among them—a woman whose heart is fashioned of pure, heavenly gold and whose spirit laughs at the very idea of growing old.

This is not just another wonderful book, my dearest friend and sister-of-my-soul. This is the living, breathing chronicle of your extraordinary life—a sacred record of how one woman, filled to overflowing with divine purpose, unshakeable will, and faith that moves mountains, has touched, transformed, and elevated countless women and men across continents.

You did not merely hand us a key; you became the master key

yourself —unlocking doors to opportunities we never dreamed

existed, to joys we had never tasted, to miracles we only discovered when we finally obeyed your gentle, persistent whisper: "Just show up, darling... God and I will do the rest."

I have never encountered generosity that flows so freely, so silently, so completely without expectation. Every breakfast, lunch, and dinner; every tank of gas on our endless California journeys; every hotel suite, every flight upgrade, every gift wrapped in love—she covered it all with a smile and a quiet "Don't even think about it." Never once did she allow gratitude to become a burden. She gives the way oceans give waves: endlessly, joyfully, because that is who she is at the very core of her being.

She is the living embodiment of the woman every woman on earth should aspire to become---confident as a lioness, radiant as dawn, always dressed to royal perfection, gliding into every room as though she still wears the Miss Universe crown she never truly laid down. Even in her golden season she walks like royalty incarnate—tall, dazzling, elegant, alive with holy fire. Age does not dim her; it burnishes her until she glows brighter than ever.

I have watched her deliberately choose the farthest parking space, then walk—slowly, gracefully, deliberately—toward her home, refusing to surrender one inch to the pain in her joints. Old age knocks daily; she pretends no one is home. While others her age retreat into silence or complaint, Dr. Robbie only multiplies her giving—more clothes from her overflowing closet, more hours from her day, more love from her inexhaustible heart, more encouragement from her lips that never speak defeat.

She serves, yet never as a servant—always as a queen dispensing favor from her throne of grace. Every single day her phone becomes a fountain of life: "Good morning, beautiful!" "Hello, my darling, I saw the sun rise and thought of you!" She has anointed more hearts with those simple words than most evangelists do in a lifetime. Her voice remains soft as silk; she only raises it when joy, worship, or holy laughter demands it. She leads with tenderness, corrects with love, persuades with heaven's own gentleness, and believes in people long after they have stopped believing in themselves.

H.R.M. Prof. Dr. Queen Eden Soriano Trinidad, Prime Minister, State of Birland
Paramount Queen Kingdom of Birland
https://birlandgovernment.com
https://edensorianotrinidad.com
https://www.facebook.com/queeneden.trinidad/
https://www.instagram.com/queen_edenstrinidad/?hl=en
https://www.youtube.com/channel/UC4fDOhealYN61BxI_xItVw?view_as=subscriber

---

Dr. B. Testimonial: "She Is My Fuel to Keep Going"

There are few people in this world whose presence alone can light up an entire room—and Lady Ambassador Robbie Motter is one of them. She is more than a mentor, more than a friend, more than a leader. Robbie is a force of nature, a living legacy, and the embodiment of unstoppable.

At nearly 90 years old, Robbie continues to show up with the same vibrant energy, passion, and commitment that she's carried for decades. She doesn't just show up for herself, she shows up for all of us. For every woman with a dream. For every leader with a voice, for every person who dares to rise.

When I feel exhausted or overwhelmed, I think of her. When I want to hide, cancel, or disappear, I picture her still showing up to events, meetings, conferences, and calls—always dressed with purpose, always speaking with power, always encouraging others to shine. It reignites something in me. She is my fuel. She is my reminder to keep going, to never give up, and to always rise with grace and grit.

Robbie doesn't just lead—she empowers. She uplifts. She connects. She creates spaces where women are seen, valued, and celebrated. She has touched thousands of lives—many of us more than once—and she never asks for anything in return. Her legacy is not just in the organizations she's built or the awards she's earned—it lives in every woman she's helped stand a little taller, speak a little louder, and believe a little more.

She helped me find my light in moments when I didn't even realize I was dimming it. Because of her, I am committed to doing the same for others. That's the real impact of her legacy. It's enduring. It multiplies.

As Robbie turns 90, I celebrate not just for what she's done, but for who she is—a living example of courage, consistency, and compassion. May we all carry her light forward, pass it on, and continue the mission she's modeled so fiercely: to rise, to serve, and to empower others—no matter our age, no matter the challenge.

Lady Robbie, you are a gift to this world. Thank you for being my light, my fuel, my friend, and my forever inspiration.

Dr. Angelica Benavides

~~~~~~~~~~~~~~~~~~~~

Lady Amb Dr. h.c. Robbie Motter! Militarily speaking, she has journeyed and progressed from a One-star General to a Four-star General! I first met Robbie in 2000 (almost 25 years ago) at the NAFE Annual Women Empowerment Conference in New York City through a mutual friend (Claudia Gilliard). I knew at that time Robbie was more than just a NAFE Global Coordinator. Robbie is a "Woman of Many Successful Adventures" who helps other women to be successful through encouragement, empowerment, knowledge sharing, and more! With the help of the Lord and through Robbie's mentoring, the 501 (C)(3) Women In Networking (WIN) Indianapolis Organization, (former network of NAFE), is thriving and is very successful.

Robbie is an extraordinary Mentor and has been mine as the Women In Networking Network Director ever since 2011, after the passing of then Director Claudia Gilliard. I called Robbie and asked, "What shall I do as Co-Director?" Robbie immediately stated, "Carry the Torch. You can do it because you're already doing it. Direct, lead, guide, succeed, and I'll help you"! She did! Instead of being in the background or being someone's sidekick, I "stepped up to the plate", created a WIN Board of Directors, and "got the ball moving".
~~~~~~~~~~~~~~~~~~~~

Robbie's mentoring has changed my life in various ways because she's not just a mentor or a leader, but one who "shows up" and supports people, globally! We invited Robbie to be our Guest Speaker for the 2017 WIN Conference. She came from California and presented one of the most powerful messages ever heard in the Midwest! The crowd was ecstatic!

Through Robbie's empowerment, I help empower others by allowing them to exert their responsibilities, trust their ideas, and provide educational opportunities through the WIN Education Scholarship Foundation for them and their children, We provide weekly Buddy Checks on their health and well-being, and monthly inspirational Chaplain's Chats. Thank you, Robbie, for everything. You're the best!

Amb. Mary Autrey

~~~~~~~~~~~~~~~~~~~~

Robbie Motter – A Beacon of Light for All Seasons and People!

Listen to leaves falling in the breeze,
and sounds of Birds Chirping in the air.
Pretty much like people enjoying Fall, Turkey, and Deer!
Now that Fall and Thanksgiving are gone,
Look! It's Winter, and snow is on, right around the corner!
Some wishing for snow; some wishing for the former!
Show Up and Show Out! Take Winter as if it's no longer!
Love it or leave it; May still show sunshine, snow and ice!
Think twice! Are we having a White Christmas? Nobody knows!
Let it snow; Wrap up warmly; Let it snow!
Staying home because of the weather? No! Show Up and Show Out!
~~~~~~~~~~~~~~~~~~~~

You never know who might be out and about!
Look around: Listen to the sounds. Now Spring and Summer are in the air!
You might see the Woman of purpose and power anywhere!
Ah! There she is -- a burst of sunshine, a light, as she surfaces everywhere!
All decked out in blue; Robbie Motter; unstoppable you!
Your virtues embody the woman in Proverbs 31:

"Wise, industrious, compassionate, strong, business acumen, faith, and wisdom."

Of course, you're "worth far more than rubies"!

Why not do another life documentary or instead make some movies?

Who can show up and show out better than you?

A woman of purpose, power, and truth, there's no one like you!

Only you, Robbie, are that woman of unstoppable faith,

Always encouraging and helping others to run the race!

Thank you.

Mary Aurtrey

Mary Aurtrey, Network Director, Women in Networking Indianapolis, GFSE Member

When I asked my friend Raziel for recommendations for networking groups, I never imagined I'd be introduced to a community that offers so much more than networking, true support, joy, and camaraderie. Since my very first event a little over a year ago, this group has opened doors I had only dreamed about: co-authoring a book, receiving an international award, meeting incredible entrepreneurs who now feel like real friends, and—something that fills my soul—a space to laugh, dress up, connect, and enjoy genuine girl time.

Robbie leads with a heart of pure gold. She goes out of her way to support everyone, including me. I'll never forget the day she called me out of the blue from Miami because she was with an influential Spanish-speaking woman and wanted us to meet. She was literally across the country... Thinking about me! And I know I'm not the only one—she shows up for everyone she knows.

Even as a relatively new member, I have felt deeply supported, seen, and welcomed. I am truly grateful for the honor of knowing her.

I have always believed that the leader sets the tone of any organization—and Robbie's golden heart attracts other golden hearts. This community is proof of that.

With gratitude and joy,

The Femelocity Team (a.k.a. Liliana)

A Legacy of Inspiration

Robbie Motter is a true guiding star and an unstoppable force of love and empowerment. Her legacy touches the lives of countless women around the world—those who have felt invisible, discarded, or broken, and who have found their voice, purpose, and strength through her unwavering dedication.

Robbie and GSFE have created a global family that lifts women from all walks of life—those unseen by society, the less confident, the ordinary women with extraordinary potential, and professional women striving to soar to new heights. She has an extraordinary gift for understanding their deepest needs, encouraging them to step beyond their comfort zones, and inspiring them to embrace all that they are destined to become.

Her work is rooted in compassion, resilience, and faith. Through her mentorship, her words, and her latest book, "She Showed Up: A Woman of Purpose, Power & Unstoppable Faith", Robbie reminds us that every woman carries a crown—symbolizing her worth, dignity, and divine potential. She teaches that confidence is earned through perseverance and that courage whispers, guiding women to step into their power.

Robbie's life is a testament to the power of showing up—despite adversity, doubts, or hardships—because she understands that every act of kindness, every connection, and every act of service creates ripples of transformation. Her legacy isn't just in her titles or achievements, but in the lives she has uplifted, inspired, and empowered to lead with love and purpose.

Robbie Motter's mission continues to ignite a movement—one woman at a time—building leaders, healing communities, and fostering a sisterhood that knows no borders. Her unwavering love, faith, and dedication serve as a reminder that every woman has a crown and a story worth telling.

Her legacy is a world where women are seen, celebrated, and empowered to show up boldly and beautifully—because Robbie demonstrated what it truly means to lead with heart.

Amb. Reverend Dr. Christine Park, DD

Director, GSFE Menifee Network

~~~~~~~~~~~~~~~~~~~~~~

I first met Robbie Motter many years ago while working for the State Assembly, and I continued to show up to her meetings and events. She played a pivotal role in helping me discover my purpose. She believed in me, encouraged me to dream bigger and overcome my fears. Thanks to her mentorship, guidance, and support, I founded MilVet, a nonprofit that has touched the lives of thousands of deployed troops, veterans, and their families.

Robbie's wisdom and leadership have truly opened doors for me, enabling me to make a meaningful impact in my community, in the lives of those I serve on a global scale, and in my family. Even after all these years, she continues to inspire and motivate me. Her influence has led to incredible achievements, including an honorary doctorate in
~~~~~~~~~~~~~~~~~~~~~~

Humanitarianism, Presidential awards, authoring books, and building a legacy rooted in giving back to others.

Robbie's story and insights in her book are a testament to the power of belief, perseverance, and compassionate leadership. I highly recommend it to anyone looking to be inspired and empowered to make a difference. Show up and ask - you will open doors to things you have never imagined, just as Robbie has shown me.

Raven Hilden

Founder/CEO MilVet.org

It is with deep gratitude and profound respect that I honor Lady Amb. Dr. Robbie Motter. She is an extraordinary mentor, connector, and force for empowerment whose influence forever changed the trajectory of my life.

Robbie saw in me what I had not yet fully seen in myself. She stopped me from playing small simply by doing what she does best: opening doors, creating connections, and calling forth greatness. She introduced me to the City Officials in Menifee and connected me with dynamic women entrepreneurs who became sisters, collaborators, and lifelong friends. Through her encouragement, I stepped into leadership and service instead of shrinking into the background.

Because of Robbie, I served with the Lions Club and in the General Federation of Women's Clubs, where I went on to

become President for two years. I was able to collaborate with
the Boys and Girls Club and MilVet. She entrusted me with
leadership in NAFE, and that pathway unfolded into becoming
the Director for GSFE Riverside. Each role expanded my voice,
my influence, and my purpose.

Robbie awakened in me a love for service and community. As
I became more involved, doors opened that I never imagined.
I received numerous awards from dignitaries and community
leaders, including the Lifetime Achievement Award from
three U.S. Presidents: President Obama, President Trump, and
President Biden. In December 2021, I received the Monthly
Citizen Award from Mayor Bill Zimmerman, and earlier that
year, the title of Ms. Elegance from the Women of Achievement
International. My journey continued with the SIMA Award
from London and an Honorary Doctorate in Humanitarianism
in 2022. These recognitions were not just achievements; they
were affirmations of the seeds Robbie planted.

And then came the moment that changed everything; Robbie
told me to tell my story. She encouraged me to write, to speak,
and to share the lessons life had taught me. Because of her belief
in me, I wrote my first book, which became a national and
international bestseller. Today, my books continue to inspire
globally, and The Power of Networking is a testament to what
Robbie taught me. The Power of Networking of Collective
Wisdom is housed in the oldest library in the world because of
her influence.

I could write volumes about what I gained from Robbie:
mentorship that stretches you, exposure that elevates you,
networking that transforms you, and life experiences that

shape the woman you become. She is a destiny-shifter, a door-opener, and a lifelong champion.

Lady Amb. Dr. Robbie Motter, thank you for seeing me, believing in me, and guiding me into the fullness of who I was meant to be. My story carries your fingerprints, and my journey is forever richer because you walked alongside me.

Amb. Dr. h.c. Joan E. Wakeland

I have known Robbie Motter for thirteen years. In that time, I've admired her enthusiasm, energy, determination, endless hours of orchestrating the GSFE events – 200%. What do we expect of a 90-year-old trailblazer, passionate achiever, and (as all my grandchildren relate to Dr. Seuss) "Oh, The Places You Go," the mountains you climb? And you will succeed: your mountain is waiting! That being said, I value our friendship with your love, laughter, our many road trips, your endless kindness, the gowns, the crowns, the certificates, and (of course) the bling! May God bless you, keep you safe, and grant you many years ahead. I ring the bell 90 times for an extraordinary woman.

Jean Olexa

"Ms. O The Organizer" your forever friend gigi8257@gmail.com

"Robbie Motter: The Unbreakable Woman Who Turned Her Pain into Power and Built a Global Sisterhood"

Reading She Showed Up is like standing in the presence of a woman whose life became a lighthouse; not because she had an easy path, but because she refused to let hardship dim her purpose. Robbie Motter's story is a powerful reminder that leadership built on integrity, compassion, and service transforms the world.

What moved me the most is the honesty of her journey. Robbie never hides the truth of her beginnings as a young girl with no support, moving from foster home to foster home, learning far too early what it meant to stand alone. Yet instead of letting those memories harden her, she allowed them to shape her into a humanitarian whose mission is to ensure no woman ever walks alone again. Her kindness comes from knowing the pain of having no one. Her courage comes from surviving storms that would have broken others. Her strength comes from refusing to give up.

Every chapter reflects her heart: showing up when she was tired, lifting women when she herself was hurting, seeing the invisible, and believing in others long before they believed in themselves. GSFE is not just an organization she created; it is her soul's calling, a global movement built from love, service, and unity. At 89, she still serves with the energy of someone who knows her purpose is far from finished.

This book is more than a memoir. It is a testimony of resilience, a guide for those who lead with love, and a celebration of a woman whose life proves that kindness creates legacies. Robbie leads with her heart, "The Robbie Way", and she reminds all of us that when we show up with purpose, we become unstoppable.

Thank you, Robbie, for being my mentor, my coach, and my true friend.

With love,

Amb. Dr. (h.c) Angeline Benjamin
Author and Motivational Speaker
Director, Virtual Thursday GSFE (Global Society for Female Entrepreneurs)
albenjamin.bb27@gmail.com
https://www.linkedin.com/in/angelinebenjamin/

~~~~~~~~~~~~~~~~~

Queen Mother, I loved the book! It's very powerful and inspiring and will surely leave a blueprint for your legacy and the impact you have made.

A ripple effect of miracles continues to unfold for women across the globe because of Queen Mother Lady Ambassador Dr. Robbie Motter — a visionary whose heart beats for service, empowerment, and generational elevation. With grace, generosity, and unwavering presence, she has

uplifted women one by one, making an impact, leaving footprints of hope, confidence, and possibility in her wake. This book is more than a story — it is a window into her purpose, her why, and the legacy she has been divinely ordained to build. Through these pages, we witness the power of one
~~~~~~~~~~~~~~~~~

woman's calling to pour out her heart and soul so others may rise. Inspiring, profoundly moving, and beautifully written, this work stands as a testament to what happens when a woman leads with love and serves with vision by just showing up!

Ambassador Dr. Doula Lakeysha Mattis h.c.
CEO, Lakeysha Mattis Enterprises
https://www.youtube.com/channel/
UCipxsaArlvzijX78GjVlbrw/about
https://www.linkedin.com/in/lakeyshamattisenterprises/
https://speakerhub.com/speaker/lakeysha-mattis
https://www.instagram.com/lakeyshamattisenterprises/?hl=en
https://www.facebook.com/lakeyshamattisenterprises/

~~~~~~~~~~~~~~~~~~~~

Surviving to Thriving

That's the Awesome Story of Robbie Motter, told in this book. From Scream to Queen, Robbie's innate intelligence, indominable spirit, and unwavering commitment to helping others has shone a light on all around her. Her autobiography begins with a little girl abandoned by her mother living in foster homes in Hawaii at the time the Japanese bombed Pearl Harbor. Then it takes us all the way to a powerful, accomplished, inspiring woman who steps on stages in Washington, London, Paris, Manila and Nairobi. At almost 90 years old, she has with several bestselling books, many honorary titles, and has a successful international nonprofit organization -- the Global Society for Female Executives (GSFE). Thousands of women around the world have been
~~~~~~~~~~~~~~~~~~~~

helped, empowered, and uplifted by Queen Lady Ambassador Dr. (h.c) Robbie Motter. She is a living legend and influencer among all who know and love her. Today, everywhere around the world, entrepreneurial women and many men hear her powerful message and her mantra, loudly resounds and draws echoes: "JUST SHOW UP, AND ASK"

Carol Liege, Founder and CEO
The Legacy Factory LLC
https://thelegacyfactory.com
https://linkedin.com/in/carolliege
https://facebook.com/carolliege

~~~~~~~~~~~~~~~~~~~~~~~

In the style of Robbie's new book, I have written my short story about said same - "Show Up... and Ask"

The first time that I Showed Up was Dec. 18, 1944.... The day I was born...and glad that I did. It made my mother's day!!

My Dad had already gone into WWII in the Pacific...but it made my older brother and sister happy also... See what showing up can do??

But it is more than Showing Up...bring something with you... your past, your present and your future! Those presents tell your full story and contain many of your Asks. Then the people that Showed up start telling you their stories...and if you listen hard enough you will detect some Asks that they did not think that they even had...but now you and they know...and you will have some thoughts/ideas/plans about their unintended Ask.
~~~~~~~~~~~~~~~~~~~~~~~

A historic Ask on my part...it was 1967, and off to the Vietnam War I go... It was the US Air Force... I wasn't told to join in... I Asked.

I needed to get out of my Home and College routine...so I asked where in the world could I go to see the world? I got my answer of course... Vietnam for 2-1/2 years. (Ask not what your Country can do for you but ask what you can do for your Country - JFK 1960). I got my answer...met people from all over the US and the World...saw and did things that I had never dreamed of...and of course in return I helped a lot of kids. The average age the US military in Vietnam was 19 years old ...did they ever have a lot of Asks!!)

Another Ask...As a lobbyist in Washington D.C., I worked with the Atlantic Richfield Oil Company (ARCO) while working on Ronald Reagan's transition Team (1980-81) I was asked to help get Jim Watt (Sec of Interior) and Any Gorsuch (Administrator Env. Protection Agency) coached to respond to all the questions they were going to get asked from their respective Congressional Appointment Hearings. Six weeks later, came results. They both got their Reagan Administration jobs...and ARCO got their Alaskan Oil Pipeline finally approved and built.

So now I have another Ask...of you and all of our GSFE friends and family...that you come to the GSFE Events with your questions of how you can expand on the work that Robbie started many years ago with GSFE (and now affiliated organizations around the world). A question that combines Showing Up with actions that will continue to open up some still closed womanly doors around the world...because as John Wayne would say "Well, sorry doesn't get 'er done, Dude".

John Connor, GSFE Ambassador
Owner, Tudor House Hotel & Restaurant, Arrowhead CA
https://www.tudorhouseentertainment.com
https://www.facebook.com/p/John-Connor-100045863917624/

~~~~~~~~~~~~~~~~~~

Testimony for a Phenomenal Woman Turning 90

Today, we honor a woman whose life has been a lighthouse for so many—especially for me. Dr. Robbie Motter, at 90 years young, she stands as proof that when a woman shows up with purpose, power, and unstoppable faith, she becomes a force that shapes lives, shifts futures, and inspires generations.

Robbie has been more than a mentor. She has been my best friend, my travel partner, my compass, and the quiet, steady whisper of faith that reminded me who I was created to be. She encouraged me to dream bigger than my fears, and she pushed me to step into spaces I once thought were unreachable.

Because of her, I became an author.

Because she believed in me, I found the courage to write—then to write again—and again.

And today, I stand as an international bestselling author with over 20 books, a legacy I never imagined for myself. She didn't just tell me I could do it—she walked beside me, lifted me, guided me, and reminded me that my voice had value and my story had power.

She encouraged me to embrace my journey to Africa, reminding
~~~~~~~~~~~~~~~~~~

me that humanitarian work is not just an act of service, it is an act of love, of purpose, of global connection. She taught me that when you give of yourself, the world gives back in ways you could never predict. She showed me that volunteerism is not an obligation, it is a blessing, a privilege, and one of life's most precious treasures.

She told me, "Keep showing up. You never know what treasures you will find."

And she was right—because every time I showed up, something inside me grew. My purpose expanded. My faith deepened. My impact widened.

The truth is, Robbie never showed up because life was simple, she showed up because faith told her she was created for more. And in doing so, she taught the rest of us that:

You are never too young,

never too old,

never too broken,

never too busy

to rise.

Every step forward—no matter how small—brings you closer to the woman you were born to be.

She has spent a lifetime showing women their strength, reminding them that their voices matter, and proving that presence alone can shift the world. She stood tall. She asked boldly. She walked with purpose. And through it all, she carried love and faith like twin pillars that held her—and all of us—up.

At 90, she remains unstoppable.

A woman of grace.

A warrior of faith.

A champion of women.

A mentor whose influence stretches across continents and generations.

Today, we celebrate her remarkable life, the countless doors she opened, the extraordinary paths she paved, and the lives—mine included—that she changed forever.

Happy 90th birthday to an unbelievable woman. May her legacy continue to shine, inspire, and remind us all to keep showing up... because the world is better every time she does, and every time we dare to follow her example.

Thank you, my friend, for everything.

With love,

Dorothy

Amb. Dr. h.c. Dorothy Wolons
Dorothy.Wolons@yahoo.com

RKMPII Ambassador of Kindness & Happiness
(h.c.) Humanitarian
MOM/Grandma
Public Speaker
Minister
New Hub Auto Service
Advanced Emission Specialist

GSFE-Global Society for Female Entrepreneurs
International Best-Selling Author-Collaboration:
It's All About Showing Up
It's All About Showing Up Volume 3
The Power of Networking
Voices of Peace
Catalyst for Change
Catalyst for Change Book 2
Catalyst for Change Book 3
Global Iconic Changemakers of the 21st Century
A Leader with a Heart of Gold
What are you Wearing?
One World, One Heart: Celebrating Peace in Diversity
What's Your Why?
Winning Women
Voices for Education: Uniting for SDG 4
Passion-Driven: Leadership-Cultivating People and Purpose for Business Growth
The Power Within: Women's Stories of Resilience and Leadership
Culture of People: Navigating Human Behavior in Organizations
The Power Within: Women's Stories of Resilience and Leadership -2
Breaking the Silence
Behind the Mask
Curriculum Revolution
The Digital Society: Reimaging Social Dynamics with Artificial Intelligence

Legacy of Light:90 years of Empowering others

~~~~~~~~~~~~~~~~

Robbie Motter is a force of leadership, mentorship, and connection. In her book, you feel the same presence she brings into every room and every life she touches: a woman who truly shows up, not only for herself, but for others, helping them grow, shine, and step boldly into their purpose.

As the founder of the Global Society for Female Entrepreneurs, Robbie has built a movement that reaches nationally and internationally, empowering women—and men—to become
~~~~~~~~~~~~~~~~

authors, entrepreneurs, artists, and leaders in their own

right. Her vision is expansive, her energy tireless, and her commitment unwavering. Robbie never rests; she is always imagining what's next—another event, another collaboration, another opportunity to uplift and recognize others.

What sets Robbie apart is her generosity of spirit. She brings people together, collaborates with organizations near and far, and intentionally creates space to celebrate kindness, excellence, and service. She sees potential where others may not, and she champions it until it flourishes.

Thank you, Robbie, for being our Queen, our leader, and our guide. You have planted a seed that continues to grow, multiply, and inspire—and it will never die.

I love you Robbie,

Amb. Dr. (h.c.) Marcy Decato
Co-Owner of Creative Solutions Marketing & Printing, Inc.

~~~~~~~~~~~~~~~~

Testimony for Dr. Robbie Motter's Book by

Dr. Verlaine Crawford (h.c) 12-20-2025

"She Showed Up: A Woman of Purpose, Power, and Unstoppable Faith" is a book for all seasons of your life. It is full of information, experience, and wisdom gained from 90 years of being on Earth that is distilled into sentences that feed your
~~~~~~~~~~~~~~~~

soul. It is the kind of book that you can ask a question and open to any page and receive a perfect answer.

Lady, Ambassador, Queen, Doctor Robbie Motter is a gentle, humble soul who truly wears a crown and receives her many titles and awards not to show off, but to demonstrate to others that a life of caring and giving can result in many blessings.

There are few people in life that can serve as a mother figure, a mentor, a sister, and a friend to so many people around the world. She serves as an anchor to keep you steady and as sails to set you free while standing as a guiding light to follow toward your goal.

The book, "She Showed Up," provides you with the recipe for success, written in such a way that each ingredient is clear, concise, and powerful! Share it with your family and friends, so that they may learn how to move forward with grace, strength, and resilience.

I met Dr. Robbie twenty years ago, and she asked me to speak at two different meeting locations for the groups of women she had gathered. She is always kind, welcoming, full of fun, good humor, and wisdom to share.

Dr. Robbie opened the door for me to receive a gladly received honorary doctorate in Humanitarianism from the Global International Advocate University. Her organization GSFE (Global Society of Female Entrepreneurs) and a marvelous sister organization, LOANI (Leaders of All Nations International), founded by Professor Carolyn Makaka, have presented me with wonderful awards that have helped to increase my confidence and also add credence for my books. Speaking about personal growth on the world stage, these distinctions have helped me to be featured in Becoming Her and Voraka magazines.

Awards gratefully received include Speaker of the Year Award from Rise to Greater Heights 2023, The 100 Women Global Leader and Role Model Award, Global Icon Author Award 2024 (A Lifetime Achievement Award for an Outstanding Contribution to Literature), Miracle Women Award 2024, Woman of the Year Award 2024, and The Unstoppable Beautiful Soul Award 2025.

My books include:
The Power of Wholeness: The Power to Manifest Health, Wealth, Love, and Self-Expression in Your Life.
 Endless Shades of the Mystical Rose: A Poetic Personal Journal of Life and Love
Emotional Healing: Experience Balance and Self-Empowerment in an Age of Rapid Change
The Heart of Transformation and the Butterfly Effect
Daughter of God: Angelic Messages of Wisdom and Love
Ending the Battle Within: How to Create a Harmonious Life by Working with Your Subpersonalities.
Plus, chapters in seven anthologies
My websites are: www.CreativeLifeAdventures.com and www.VerlaineCrawford.com
Email: VerlaineCrawford@gmail.com

I met Robbie Motter in 2001 when I assumed the role of President, National Association for Female Executives (NAFE). The organization was founded in 1973 and focused on the success of women in business -- both as entrepreneurs and as corporate employees – and had 125,000 members with NAFE affiliate networks in every state. I soon learned that the largest of these networks (actually a network of networks) thrived in California under Robbie's leadership. Robbie first showed up in my life at a NAFE conference in New York sporting a big blue hat and lighting up the room. I didn't know what to make of her but soon recognized a true original and a force for women's success. Several years later, NAFE honored her with a Woman of Excellence Award for Mentorship, and I know no one who has mentored as many, building women's confidence with her tireless support. Indefatigable back then and still today with her 90th birthday, she continues to engender my awe and immeasurable respect. I still cherish the joyful surprise I felt when I arrived at one of her conference sites as a keynote speaker and walked to a birthday party she had orchestrated for me. What makes Robbie such an original is not just the boundless heart she brings into every room, and it's not just her extraordinary ability to connect the hearts of the wide circle of women she engages with, it's also the depth of her commitment to bringing out the best in us all. And here's my favorite Robbie-ism: "Show up anyway!"

Betty Spence, Ph.D., retired Head of Women's Advancement, Sera mount

I've known Robbie Motter for a few decades.

She carries with her an impeccable sense of servitude, knowledge, and experience.

In a world where many people are opportunistic, she shares openly her skills and knowledge, transforming lives from every area on her journey.

A truly rare human being.

Jim Lutes,

CEO Lutes International

~~~~~~~~~~~~~~~~~~~~~~

Dr. Robbie Motter embodies the very spirit of generosity and sisterhood she writes about in She Showed Up.

A few years ago, as a member of GSFE, I experienced firsthand the depth of her kindness when she opened her home to me, renting me a room and allowing me to film portions of my movie Who's Gonna Take Care of Me? there. Robbie not only played the role of Helen Watson, but she also reached out to her vast GSFE network, helping secure a member's beautiful home for filming and connecting me with other members for speaking and extra roles in the future when funding allows.

While being her roommate, I witnessed her weekly trips to thrift stores—not for herself, but to buy clothes for friends and members. She shared meals with me, texting me there was a delicious leftover in the fridge because she could only eat half.
~~~~~~~~~~~~~~~~~~~~~~

She gave me dresses, jewelry, shoes, etc., and even let me rent her car once a month. Robbie's beautiful heart is boundless. Her generosity and spirit of service embody everything GSFE stands for. Because of her, I've made lifelong friends and witnessed what true sisterhood looks like.

Special Note: The 2 hour portion of my film featuring Robbie and GSFE member Chebra Dorsey in acting roles will be showcased at major film festivals when I complete postproduction this coming summer. 35 professional actors and entertainers are in the film, and some GSFE members are producers on the film, and their names will appear in the end credits.

—Marneen Fields, Award-winning filmmaker, scriptwriter, SAG actress, composer, singer, author, and former Hollywood stuntwoman.

https://www.imdb.me/marneenfields

"If ever there was a person who 'walked her talk' about Showing Up, it is Lady Robbie Motter!

Robbie shows up to everything, large and small, and has taught us all in GSFE that there is a "Diamond" waiting for you each time you go!- And that is so true.

Also, Robbie has showed up for each one of us, quite often, in ways no one else has!- Robbie has shown up for me in recommending me for my Sue Talk in 2021, and then came to the taping. Come to think of it, she has shown up for me in so many places and situations that I will never forget.

I also enjoy seeing how she shows up so so many other GSFE members and people around the world!

When you have been touched by Robbie, you have been held by an angel! Barbara A. Berg- The Ring Shui Lady- And yes, Robbie has been my biggest supporter in Ring Shui-

She has helped me bring this concept to so many women whom I know and don't know in so many places!

I wouldn't have the life I have if Robbie hadn't shown up for me, and so many other women and men.

From Barbara Berg

~~~~~~~~~~~~~~~~~~~~~~

I met our beloved Dr. Robbie at a Women's Leadership Conference in Riverside, California in August of 2024. She looked stunning as ever, and I happened to sit down beside her, never realizing that this single moment would change the trajectory of my entire life. She immediately inspired me, offering a powerful pep talk about the importance of showing up fully and with radiant confidence. In that first conversation, I invited her to come try Jack's Bar-B-Q in Lake Elsinore, California, where I work. In turn, she shared with me the calendar of events for the Global Society for Female Entrepreneurs and invited me to join. When I visited the website, I was filled with awe at the impact she has
~~~~~~~~~~~~~~~~~~~~~~

made in countless lives around the world. She is an absolute powerhouse, truly superhuman in her determination, grace, and purpose-driven leadership.

On May 5th, 2025, I invited her to the restaurant to celebrate her Visionary Leadership. I wanted to honor her for the extraordinary impact she continues to make in the world. I purchased all of her books and felt an overwhelming sense of wonder when she shared that the books would be placed in the Library of Alexandria in Egypt. As a librarian of nine years, this was a dream come true, one I never even imagined was possible.

I was honored to contribute to the book What's Your Why, and through her, I was introduced to Raymond Banzuela of International Publications. That connection led me to add my chapters to ten more books in 2025 alone. My grandmother is the same age as Dr. Robbie and always wanted me to write a book. I feel so blessed that I was able to make that wish come true thanks to this precious connection.

I have deeply loved our time together throughout the year. Painting in Arrowhead, attending gatherings, and teaching workshops have brought me immense joy. I will never forget when she picked me up for my first workshop on artificial intelligence, titled Harnessing AI for Visionary Leadership. As she shared her schedule, I remember wishing I had her energy and stamina! I was also deeply inspired by her experiences in Africa and am profoundly proud of all that she has accomplished in the world.

Dr. Robbie was a VIP foreword author for the book I also contributed to called A Legacy in Humanitarianism, Journeys to Genuine Connections Through Purpose, People, and Passion further reflecting her unwavering commitment to service. Her story is so inspiring and she empowers and uplifts us all. I cherish her weekly positive messages and videos sharing her guiding light.

The International Kindness Event brought me tremendous joy. She worked tirelessly making it a fabulous event full of goodness and joy. The Goddess calendar is amazing, and the glamour photos made me feel like a movie star. I was deeply honored to receive an International Peace Award, an acknowledgment that meant the world to me. I was also blessed with the Unstoppable Beautiful Souls Award, and in that moment, I knew I had truly found my tribe. Through these experiences, I finally met the legendary Dr. Caroline Makaka of Leaders of All Nations International. When she invited me to join the Zoom calls, tears streamed down my face. I have always cherished the vision of people from all over the world gathering in peace, sharing goodness, and serving others together. Seeing this dream realized has been nothing short of miraculous.

We had our live holiday party at Jack's and we did a lottery pool since it was going over a billion dollars. So far we are still in the game three weeks later. We won $9 last week and nobody has won the big Powerball yet. I had printed out a sheet that had us list our wishes: something for yourself, something for someone you love and something for your legacy in the community. I believe that our group is exactly who should win the lottery together. We will do incredible things together no matter what; but the funding would be such a gift to the entire world.

My life is genuinely brighter, more connected, and my career has aligned me EXACTLY where I am meant to be. I pray that I can pay it forward because that is exactly what she would want. I am sending Dr. Robbie endless love and gratitude. She is the greatest professional mentor of my life. God bless our precious Queen. We love you and I can't wait to see what's next!

Amb. Stephanie Lynn

~~~~~~~~~~~~~~~~~

To say that Ambassador Dr. H.C. Robbie Motter has shown up would be a profound understatement. For nearly five decades, Robbie has been a visionary force in women's leadership—building platforms, forging global networks, and creating opportunities where none previously existed.

What makes *She Showed Up* so compelling is that it is both a leadership playbook and a deeply personal testimony. Robbie doesn't just talk about influence—she demonstrates how it is earned through consistency, courage, and the willingness to ask. This book is a masterclass in how one person's clarity of purpose, paired with relentless follow-through, can grow into a global enterprise of ideas, relationships, and impact.

As the founder and creator of the Global Society for Female Entrepreneurs, Robbie didn't simply build an organization—she architected a movement. One rooted in strategic connection, shared wisdom, and the understanding that when women collaborate rather than compete, the impact is exponential. Long before "community" became a business focused endorsement for *She Showed Up. *
~~~~~~~~~~~~~~~~~

buzzword, Robbie was doing the real work: bringing women together across industries, cultures, and borders, and giving them permission to lead boldly.

Having spent decades building mission-driven work myself, I recognize the rare combination of vision and execution that Robbie embodies. *She Showed Up* is not about waiting for permission or perfect timing—it is about showing up fully, trusting your voice, and understanding that leadership begins the moment you decide to take responsibility for the world you want to help shape.

This is a must-read for entrepreneurs, executives, and changemakers who want to build something that lasts—and who understand that true success is measured not only by what you create, but by who you bring with you along the way.

— Melissa Hull

Author of *Dear Drew: Creating a Life Bigger Than Grief*

Entrepreneur

Robbie Motter is the kind of woman who doesn't just talk about showing up; she lives it!

She Showed Up is more than a book; it's a reminder of what happens when women choose courage over comfort and presence over perfection. Robbie has a rare gift for making you feel seen, supported, and capable, all at the same time. Her kindness, love, and genuine care for others isn't just something she teaches; it's something every woman who works with her experiences firsthand. This book is a call to rise, to stay in the game when it gets hard, and to show up for your life with heart and purpose. I'm incredibly grateful to know Robbie, and I'm even more grateful that she shared this message with the world.

— Dr. Coach Mikki St. Germain, (HC), Author, Speaker, Podcast host, Football Coach

"Robbie has been a true inspiration to those around her, encouraging us to be our best. She leads by example demonstrating principles for empowerment that allow us to achieve our goals and enjoy success. Robbie's book shares those power principles with us."

-Bill Zimmerman
Mayor, City of Menifee 2018-2025

"She Showed Up is the book to read for success! Robbie's dynamic ability to tell it like it is and empower others to do the same is THE formula for success"!

Jill Lublin, Media magnet, 4x Best Selling author and International Speaker JillLublin.com

Can you believe Robbie Motter is almost 90?

And she's still driving all over the place, still traveling the world. Thank God she can—because she is one of my dearest friends, my mentor, and one of the strongest rocks in my garden. Besides my mother, I've never met anyone who has had such a profoundly positive impact on my life.

With all that she has done—and continues to do—Robbie keeps telling me she's going to live well past 100, traveling, driving, and spreading goodness and insight wherever she goes. And I believe her.

She has truly changed my life. I cannot thank God enough for the work she has done—and continues to do—in this world. Her books are extraordinary. The younger generation needs to dip into them, because her words are pure magic. Her heart is filled with an abundance of love, and she is beyond incredible as a leader.

I met her one day sitting in a room full of amazing women, and she stood out to me like a flame—an incredible fire of wisdom. I couldn't help myself; I had to go up and introduce myself. I wanted to know her.

And let me tell you something—this is the kind of person everyone needs in their life.

Thank you, Robbie, for all you've done for all of us. I have learned so much from you. I cannot wait for your next book.

"She Showed Up"

Peggy McIntaggart Seagren
- People come into your Life for a Reason A Season or a Lifetime -

How Dr. Robbie Has Impacted My Life

I remember the first time I met Dr. Robbie. It was at a fashion show and awards ceremony hosted by Coach Tee Lee. Her presence was striking—poised, elegant, and unmistakably that of a proper lady. She carried herself with a quiet authority that immediately commanded respect.

During our first conversation, we spoke about the power of writing a book and the importance of telling one's story. I shared with her that writing a book had always been a dream of mine. Without hesitation, she looked at me and said, "That's something you absolutely can do."

That moment of belief shifted something deep within me.

At the time, I was navigating a season where another mentor in my life was constantly telling me what I couldn't do—questioning my vision and dismissing my goals as unrealistic as I worked to build the Love and Light Movement. Dr. Robbie's encouragement stood in stark contrast. She didn't see limitations; she saw possibility.

Anytime you tell Dr. Robbie that you want to do something, she immediately steps into the role of an encourager. She not only speaks life into your dreams but actively connects you with people who can help bring those dreams into reality.

Since joining the Global Society of Female Entrepreneurs, I've learned how powerful it is to be supported by a leader like Dr. Robbie. Through her encouragement, I didn't just publish my story once—I have now contributed to four different books. Each time, I think about the power of what can happen when someone truly believes in you.

Dr. Robbie has been more than a mentor to me; she has been a friend—especially as I've navigated my healing journey while living with a brain injury. I have never been met with limitations by her. Instead, she models what it looks like to continue showing up and getting things done with grace, regardless of what life brings.

The Global Society of Female Entrepreneurs has changed my life because, for the first time, I experienced genuine kindness and true sisterhood within a community of women. Moving from being a chapter member to becoming a director empowered me to step into leadership in a feminine way—one that honors all of my gifts and allows me to serve other women, which has always been one of my deepest goals.

The mentor who once tried to tear me down taught me exactly the kind of leader I never want to be. Dr. Robbie, on the other hand, is the embodiment of the leader I aspire to become: feminine, elegant, classy, and full of life.

I am continually amazed that at 89 years old, she is still driving, moving, serving, and leading at a pace that leaves me in awe. The way she shows up in the world inspires me to keep going, to continue healing, and to trust the power of movement. Simply being in her presence—attending meetings and events alongside her—has reminded my body what is possible.

Watching how she dresses gives me permission to fully embrace my most elegant self. Her support throughout my pageant journey, including traveling with her to Las Vegas to receive my honorary doctorate, has helped shape who I am today.

I also admire how fearlessly she embraces change—whether

that's adopting new technologies like AI or encouraging women to evolve and expand. Her willingness to grow reminds us that leadership has no expiration date.

Through her example, I hope to continue becoming the kind of leader who uplifts other women, places them in the right rooms, and connects them with kindness—so they can use their gifts and show up in the world as their authentic selves.

I truly feel that Dr. Robbie has become a second mother to me, guiding me as I navigate new territory as the first female entrepreneur in my family. Because of her life, her legacy, and the connections I've made through the Global Society of Female Entrepreneurs, I know my life and my business will flourish—simply through the power of her encouragement and the example she sets.

Love and Light, Briana Rice

~~~~~~~~~~~~~~~~~~

"Absolutely inspirational—like the woman herself! This book is a masterclass in leadership and worth; it is more than a guide, it's a permission slip to recognize your own greatness. If you want to lead with heart and purpose, start here.

For 15 years, Robbie has been a mentor to me and a global champion for thousands of others around the world. I've seen her transform lives at events, or simply by making a woman feel seen. She understands that we often lead through storms with nothing but willpower, and in these pages, she provides the 'emotional lifeline' we need to keep going."
~~~~~~~~~~~~~~~~~~

Nadine Lajoie, B.Sc., #1 Best Selling Author, International, Business Manager
www.NadineRacing.com

~~~~~~~~~~~~~~~~~

She Showed Up: A Woman of Purpose, Power & Unstoppable Faith

Reading She Showed Up felt like sitting across from Robbie Motter while she shared her life, not to impress, but Sto remind you what's possible when a woman leads with heart, faith, and unwavering presence. This book is deeply moving, beautifully honest, and profoundly inspiring.

What touched me most is the way Robbie tells her story without polishing the pain or minimizing the triumph. She shows us that purpose is often born in the hardest seasons, and that true leadership isn't about titles or recognition, it's about showing up, again and again, for yourself and for others. Her life is living proof that kindness, service, and belief in women can create a ripple effect that spans generations and continents.

This is not just a memoir. It's a blueprint for impact. A reminder that you don't need to be perfect, fearless, or fully ready, you just need to be willing to show up. Robbie's story will leave you feeling seen, strengthened, and called to rise into your own purpose with courage and compassion.
~~~~~~~~~~~~~~~~~

I closed this book feeling inspired, grounded, and deeply grateful for women like Robbie Motter who lead with love and remind us that our presence matters more than we know.

Wendy Barr
Founder & CEO, Women's Business Link™

~~~~~~~~~~~~~~~~~~~~~

A TRIBUTE TO THE ICONIC ROBBIE MOTTER

It is with deep admiration and heartfelt gratitude that we offer this testimonial for the incomparable, iconic Queen Lady Ambassador Dr. Robbie Motter. Dr. Robbie is the embodiment of selfless love and unwavering support, touching the lives of others with her generous spirit every single day. Her mission to foster true sisterhood among women is both inspiring and transformative as she strives to build a world where women are connected, empowered, and uplifted.

Despite the adversities she faced growing up in foster homes, Dr. Robbie's resilience and positive outlook have shaped her into a fearless trailblazer. She walks with pride yet is grounded in remarkable humility, always ready to extend a helping hand to those in need. Her ability to encourage courage and never discourage others is a testament to her extraordinary character.

Recognizing the need for women to support one another, Dr. Robbie established the Global Society for Female Entrepreneurs, a visionary organization that now connects international women, enabling them to realize their dreams and thrive together in powerful teams. Her mantra of "showing
~~~~~~~~~~~~~~~~~~~~~

up and asking" has not only fueled her own success but has inspired countless others to pursue new horizons with confidence.

On a personal note, Dr. Robbie has played some major roles in the life of my husband Masood and me. The three of us have traveled to three continents (Europe, Asia, and Africa) to share and celebrate major milestones in our lives with LOANI (Leaders of All Nations International), GIA (Global International Alliance) and her incredible GSFE organization. Masood and I have received prestigious awards from GSFE we will forever treasure. We have been honored guests in her lovely California home several times. She is the greatest, most generous hostess. She arranged our beautiful wedding decorations at Lake Arrowhead, California, on April 21, 2023, gifted us our wedding cake, and honored us as one of my bridesmaids. This wonderful lady has become family to us as she has become for countless other people. She has openly and lovingly accepted us into her "family" circle, a true blessing for Masood and me.

Therefore, as Dr. Robbie celebrates her 90th year of excellence, we honor her legacy of service, leadership, genuine friendship, and compassion. The world is truly better because of her tireless advocacy towards women's empowerment and her genuine humanitarian spirit. She is a true friend, a huge part of our "extended" family, a woman of the highest integrity, and a one-of-a-kind trailblazer who continues to make an indelible impact. Thank you, dear Robbie, for all you do. Masood and I love you dearly and wish you many more years of happiness, health, and success. God bless you always!

Ambassador Dr. (hc) Randi D. Ward (Bhalli) and Ambassador
Dr. (hc) Chaudhry Masood Mahmood Bhalli, Owners of RM
Infinite (OneStop Possibilities)

~~~~~~~~~~~~~~~~~~~~~

Such a Beautiful View
Two Portuguese girls on an island far away
Met and became sisters and friends 'til this very day.

Sixty-two years ago, I met Robbie. I was 10, she was 13,
and we loved each other from day one.
While she organized the Boys Basketball Team with the
manager,
I was the only girl on the Boys team.
Oooooh! What Fun!

She was thoughtful and friendly and even then,
organized everything and made things right.
I was also thoughtful and friendly but very boy crazy
whenever they were in sight.

Knowing Robbie is like finding out you're going to Disneyland,
you're excited whenever she's around.
Having her friendship in my life is part of the happiness I have
found.

Life gives us moments to build on when another soul becomes a
friend.
Sure feels good knowing this deep inside, Dear Robbie,
~~~~~~~~~~~~~~~~~~~~~

as life takes us round the bend.

The path of life that I've been blessed with has such a beautiful view!
Some people go a lifetime and never experience having a special friend
like you.

Love forever,

Gail Martin
We Remember

~~~~~~~~~~~~~~~~~~~~

Dr. Lady Robbie Motter is a truly inspirational guide and mentor. She has a drive and ambition that is unsurpassed by anyone else I have met who is entering their 9th decade. In her life, she has accomplished much...and in all she has done, she has been mindful of how to bring others along. She is always creating pathways, opportunities, and chances for other entrepreneurs to shine their light, their talents, their gifts, and their genius in many different ways. Whether it is singing on stage, attending a book signing, seeing their name in lights, being recognized for the work they do...Robbie is constantly seeking opportunities for those who are connected to her many different endeavors.

I first met Robbie in March of 2023 at a book signing...I had been following GSFE for a few years on social media and I
~~~~~~~~~~~~~~~~~~~~

loved the dressing up for self, I loved the glitz and glitter of the events, and I loved the energy of the group. I knew a few people who were a part of GSFE, and I called and asked if I could attend the book signing. I was hooked at the first meeting by all of the positive energy, the singing, the dancing, and the fun. Robbie's events are truly a catalyst for entrepreneurs from all different fields to show up, be seen, and move forward.

Lady Motter is the grand dame...the one who shows up, not only for herself, but for all of the members of the Global Society of Female Entrepreneurs (GSFE). It is my honor and pleasure to know Robbie and be a part of this wonderful and beautiful organization. Robbie not only teaches us how important it is to show up, she leads by example...her life is truly her message.

With love and gratitude,
Zulmara Maria Teixeira de Lima
zulmaramaria.com
Zulmara Maria (FB: https://www.facebook.com/zulmara.maria.2025)
Zulmara Maria (Insta: https://www.instagram.com/zulmara.maria/)

~~~~~~~~~~~~~~~~~

Tribute to Lady Amb. Dr. h.c. Robbie Motter

Today we come together to honor the extraordinary life and legacy of Lady Robbie Motter, a trailblazer, an inspiring leader, and the visionary founder of the Global Society for Female Entrepreneurs (GSFE) a 501(c) (3) global nonprofit.
~~~~~~~~~~~~~~~~~

Her commitment to uplifting women and empowering communities has transformed communities, lives, including my own.

Lady Robbie Motter dedicated her life to creating opportunities for women and the globe, believing firmly in the potential of every individual to make a difference.

Through GSFE, she championed initiatives that provided education, resources, and support to women seeking to realize their dreams. Her tireless efforts not only fostered personal growth but also ignited social change, as she encouraged women to break barriers and pursue their passion fearlessly.

The impact of Lady Robbie Motter's work extends far beyond statistics and programs; it is felt in the stories of empowerment and resilience that she helped cultivate. She created a safe space for women to share their experiences, learn from one another, and build lasting connections. Her unwavering belief in the power of community inspired many to take both steps towards their goals, instilling in us the courage to dream bigger.

On a personal level, Lady Robbie Motter has profoundly influenced my life and future. Her mentorship and guidance have been invaluable, shaping my aspirations and encouraging me to pursue paths I never thought possible. Through her teachings, I learned the importance of confidence, perseverance, and the strength that comes from supporting one another.

Lady Robbie, infectious passion, and determination are sources of motivation for everyone who is fortunate enough to know her. She taught us that every challenge is an opportunity for growth, and that we are stronger together

Her legacy inspires me to carry forward her mission of empowerment, and I am committed to making a positive impact in the lives of others, just as she did for me.

As we celebrate Lady Robbie Motter's remarkable contributions, let us remember her not only for her achievements but also for her incredible spirit and compassion. May we honor her memory by embodying her values and continuing her work of empowering women and creating positive change in our communities.

Thank you, Lady Robbie Motter, for your unwavering dedication, your inspiring vision, and the profound impact you have made in our lives, your legacy will forever live on in the hearts of many around the world and continue to inspire many.

With highest respect and admiration.
Ambassador Dr.(h.c.) Charmaine Summers
Director, Lake Arrowhead network,
Senior Advisory committee member, City of Menifee, Ca.

~~~~~~~~~~~~~~~~~~~~

I have known Lady Amb. Dr. (h.c) for 18 years. She is like the Energizer Bunny that never stops.

She is always creating and producing amazing events that promote and honor others.

She has always supported me and my career over the years as I have supported hers.
~~~~~~~~~~~~~~~~~~~~

If I have learned anything from her it is that you always show up because you never know what treasure is waiting.

She has honored me with many awards for my humanity works and for that I am eternally

grateful. She is a force of nature.

Prince Fleet Easton
fleeteaston@yahoo.com
Facebook....Prince Fleet Easton
Instagram....princefleeteaston123

~~~~~~~~~~~~~~~~~

"She Showed Up! A Woman of Purpose, Power and Grace"

When I first learned about the Global Society for Women (GSFE), I had no idea how profoundly the organization would reshape my life. I was at a crossroad, excited about the possibilities ahead but uncertain about how to step into the role I felt called to fulfill. That's when I met Lady Amb Dr. Robbie Motter —the extraordinary woman whose energy, wisdom, and unwavering belief in "showing up" became the catalyst for my own transformation.

I still remember the first day we gathered in California, a sun drilled home buzzing with ambitious women from every corner of the world. From the moment she walked into the room, her presence was both grounding and electrifying. She greeted each of us with a genuine smile, a warm hug, and a simple, powerful question: "What are you here to create?" In that instant, I felt
~~~~~~~~~~~~~~~~~

seen—not just as a participant, but as a vital part of a larger story.

Over the next few days, she poured herself into our mentoring sessions. She shared stories of her own setbacks, laughed at her missteps, and, most importantly, modelled what it means to show up fully—authentically and without apology. She taught us to lean into discomfort, to ask the hard questions, and to celebrate the small victories that often go unnoticed. Her encouragement was relentless; when doubt crept in, she would lean over and whisper, "You are exactly where you need to be. Keep showing up."

Those words became my mantra.

Because of her mentorship, I began to see myself not as a passive observer but as an active creator of my destiny. I started taking the projects I had been hesitating to launch, speaking up in meetings, and stepping into leadership roles I once thought were out of reach. The ripple effect was immediate— my confidence grew, my relationships deepened, and my professional opportunities expanded in ways I could never have imagined.

What truly sets her apart is the way she lifts others while staying humble. She celebrates each person's unique path, never comparing journeys but instead highlighting the strengths each of us brings to the table. Her support isn't a oneoff gesture; it's a continuous thread that weaves through every challenge and triumph. She has become a trusted confidante, a mentor, and, frankly, a friend who I know I can call on at any hour.

To anyone reading this—whether you are just beginning your journey or you're already walking the path—know that the impact of a single person who believes in you can be transformative. She showed up for us, and in doing so, taught us to show up for ourselves and for each other. Because of her, I am a better version of myself, and I am committed to paying that gift forward.

With heartfelt gratitude,
Dr. Adaobi Cornelia Onyekweli Bakare
Founder & CEO, FamilyMediatorCroydon
Linkedin: https://www.linkedin.com/in/cornelia-adaobi-onyekweli-729b1318b/
Email: FAMILYMEDIATORCROYDON@GMAIL.COM
Website: www.familymediatorcroydon.com

~~~~~~~~~~~~~~~~~~~~~~~~~~

Lady Robbie Motter Testimonial

I am, indeed, a very fortunate woman to know this amazing soul! Her extraordinary skills, and love for assisting women to move forward and become successful entrepreneurs, has helped them to live abundantly within a community of other women soaring to heights they did not know they could accomplish.

I've known her for several decades, and when I lived in Los Angeles, she was always inviting to the next gathering of women she was creating. I could just hear in my spirits, "just show up!" No matter what I might've been doing, that call from her sincere and loving invitation was more than any of us could bear and we just had to 'show up!' Whenever we did, it was always a delightful event and exchange with other amazing
~~~~~~~~~~~~~~~~~~~~~~~~~~

women. She is a magnet for amazing women like herself. I was fortunate to even have the opportunity to be invited to stay at her own home after I was recovering from a major surgery. She said, "you take the master bedroom I'll stay in the atrium." Her generosity knew no bounds!

Those of us that know her have a sweeter life, have learned to live more graceful and elegant lives, and to never show up anywhere without being decked out as much as possible, which made it even more fun! To this day, I still dress up and think of her as I'm putting my outfits together. I love seeing her ongoing glow and spectacular wardrobe and presentations of her eternal beauty! She is and has always been our role model and I love her dearly! Even though I live far away now on the other side of the country, the imprint she has made in my life is permanent and it is called LOVE! (Maybe there are GSFE women in Boone NC?)

Ms. Jeannie Fitzsimmons, CEO, www.Awakenedheart.com Transformational "letting go" releasing coach, Reverend Bestselling Author, ASCAP composer, healing music producer, pro voiceover artist, mandala artist and poet. Jeanniefitzsimmons@gmail.com

"The ongoing unfolding of an awakened heart is a fragrant flower blessing everyone as its petals continue opening."

She Showed Up: A Woman of Purpose, Power & Unstoppable Faith

She Showed Up: A Woman of Purpose, Power & Unstoppable Faith is not merely a book—it is a living testament to what happens when a woman chooses purpose over fear and service over self. In these pages, Robbie Motter does far more than share her life story; she offers her heart, her faith, and her unwavering belief in humanity.

What makes this book extraordinary is its authenticity. Robbie's journey—from a childhood marked by abandonment and adversity to a life devoted to lifting others—is shared with humility, grace, and profound wisdom. Her story reminds us that leadership is not forged in comfort, but in courage, consistency, and compassion. She shows us that true power lies not in titles or recognition, but in the ability to show up for others, again and again, even when life is hard.

As a reader, I was deeply moved by the clarity of Robbie's mission: to ensure that no woman ever feels alone. Through her work, her words, and her example, she demonstrates that when one woman believes in herself, she creates space for countless others to rise. Her life's work through GSFE stands as a global reflection of servant leadership—where empowerment, kindness, and faith guide every action.

This book speaks directly to women who may feel unseen, unheard, or uncertain of their worth. It gently reminds them that simply showing up can change the trajectory of a life. Robbie's message is both comforting and challenging: your presence matters, your story matters, and your purpose is still unfolding.

She Showed Up is more than a memoir; it is a call to action. It invites each of us to reflect on how we show up in our own lives and how we might serve the world with greater intention, courage, and love. Robbie Motter's legacy is not confined to these pages—it lives on in the lives she has touched across generations and continents.

This book is a gift. And so is the woman who wrote it.

Dr. Jaya Sajnani, Philanthropist
Director, London UK GSFE Network
CEO and founder of Global Talent Solution Hub and YG Travel Ltd, UK

About the Testimony Author

Dr. Jaya Sajnani is an academic leader, global education advocate, and champion of women's empowerment. As CEO and Founder of Global Talent Solution Hub, she is dedicated to advancing access, equity, and international education. Her work spans academia, global leadership, and humanitarian initiatives, with a focus on education as a transformative force for individuals and communities worldwide.

~~~~~~~~~~~~~~~~~~~~

"She Is Loved By Many And Appreciated By Even More!"

I have known Robbie Motter for about 20 years, I remember going to her 80th birthday party and maybe even her 75th. She is the most amazing lady, with more energy and enthusiasm than just about anyone else I have ever known. She cares about
~~~~~~~~~~~~~~~~~~~~

others deeply, she is loved by many and appreciated by even more.

She has been a huge influence in so many lives. She is a positive, energetic, wonderful person who cares for others all the time. I don't think she realizes how much she has changed lives over the years, or maybe she does. I so appreciate the many years of friendship, guidance and just feeling her energy and love. Robbie, you are the most amazing lady! It is a joy to call you a friend and a mentor. I look forward to the next 10 years.

Aggie Kobrin

~~~~~~~~~~~~~~~~~~

Robbie Gives Me Constant Drive And Inspiration To Dream Bigger!

Having Dr. Robbie Motter in my life gives me constant drive and inspiration to dream bigger, to stay in service, and to remember that we are truly capable of fulfilling everything we desire when we lead with purpose and heart.

Robbie is soon to be 90 years old, and yet she carries more strength, clarity, and vitality than most people half her age. Her energy is contagious. Her commitment to serving women, to being a bridge of light, hope, and possibility in the world, is beyond inspiring; it is embodied wisdom in motion.

As the founder and CEO of Global Society for Female Entrepreneurs (GSFE), she has created far more than an organization. She has built a global community rooted in
~~~~~~~~~~~~~~~~~~

support, leadership, and conscious service. I have had the honor of serving alongside her—being on stage together, traveling together, and contributing to the vision she holds so beautifully. Through every experience, her integrity, generosity, and unwavering purpose shine through.

The support she has extended to LOANI, and to so many women around the world, speaks volumes about who she is: a true leader who lifts others as she rises. Having Robbie in my life expands what I believe is possible, not just professionally, but as a human being.

Thank you, Robbie Motter, for the profound impact you continue to have on my heart and in my life. Having you as a leader, a mentor, and a friend is one of the greatest gifts I could ever dream of. Thank you for your leadership and your servant heart.

Val Alino, Life Coach & Conscious Leadership Mentor
International Keynote Speaker | Author | Founder, Val Alino Coach

"A Trailblazing Force In The World Of Female Entrepreneurship"

Lady Ambassador Dr. CEO Robbie Motter of Global Society of Female Entrepreneurs serves and continues to do so at 90 years old. She serves as an inspiration to thousands of women around the globe -- including myself – she is the meaning of showing up.

I met Robbie in the Summer of 2017. She popped up on my Facebook page, and there she was, awarding women promoting the acceleration and advancement of women in business from all over the world for their contribution and dedication to their passion. I thought, "Wow, how incredible is that? I've not only met this incredible woman but witness the lives she's changing and empowering."

It wasn't until I met Robbie myself in late 2017 and got to know her better. I found out our paths are aligned. It is true, like she always says, "Showing up is like a treasure map, you never know what you're going to find." Today, her inspiration has guided me personally and professionally. Showing up first for myself, even when finding excuses not to, and realize there's no growth in that.

Robbie Motter is a trailblazing force in the world of female entrepreneurship. For decades, she's championed women's empowerment and inspired countless individuals, men and women to pursue their passions. Her unwavering commitment to 'showing up' serves as a powerful reminder that growth and opportunity await those who take action.

As we enter 2026, let Robbie's remarkable journey motivate you to embrace new challenges, support others, and create your own treasure map of success.

Let her dedication to empowering women and her mantra of "showing up" inspire you. It's amazing how one person can make such a significant impact on so many lives and you can too by showing up. As we begin a new year, her story encourages us to be brave, take risks, and pursue our dreams, just as she has done. Let's all strive to follow in her footsteps and make a positive difference in the world by SHOWING UP!

Now here we are in 2026, a new year, new beginnings. In closing, let me ask you. How are you going to show up this year for yourself? Take risks, find more reasons to say yes to your dreams. You got this!

Shelly Rufin, 33-Year College Consultant, FAFSA Expert
EDFIN College Planning
www.edfincollegeplanningexperts.com

~~~~~~~~~~~~~~~~~~

Impact Begins With Boldness!

We are Nick and Dana Haselum, a husband and wife team. We are motivational speakers, authors, and life coaches. As a couple who are passionate speaking about purpose, partnership, and showing up fully, GSFE and its founder, Lady Amb Dr. Robbie Motter met us right where we are and stretched us beyond where we thought we could go. Through its core principle, 'Showing Up', GSFE has reminded us that purpose isn't something you wait for permission to get; it's something you answer when called. GSFE has challenged us to examine how we show up not only for each other, but for the goals we've set for ourselves.

Through Dr. Motter's inspirational actions and the powerful work of GSFE, we were reminded that impact begins with boldness—to ask, to step forward, and to believe bigger
~~~~~~~~~~~~~~~~~~

than our fears. The work of GSFE reignited something in us: the confidence to dream out loud again and the confidence to ask for what aligns with our purpose. 'Showing up' isn't just a message for women—it's a call to anyone ready to live intentionally, love fully, and rise with power and grace. We are better, braver, and more aligned because of it.

To those reading this wonderful book. Your presence matters. Your voice matters. Your "yes" matters. Don't wait for the perfect moment or the right validation. Show up anyway. Ask anyway. Believe anyway. When you choose to walk in purpose with power and grace, you give others permission to do the same—and that is how lives are transformed.

If you would like to connect with us, we would love to connect with you.

Dana and Nick Haselum
Email: dana2inspire@gmail.com
Facebook: https://www.facebook.com/Dana2Inspire/

"A Living Legacy Of Love In Motion"

Robbie is a living legacy of love in motion—the rarest gem, glittering brighter than Gatsby, turning every day into a celebration styled in purpose, power and grace.

Nearly 90 years young, she's a fierce, fabulous force of nature who lifts every room she enters. She believes in people before they believe in themselves—and because of that, she doesn't just touch lives, she transforms them.

Born with a heart of gold and what feels like endless hands, she gives without limits—of her time, her home, her heart. Her generosity isn't an act; it's who she is.

"She Showed Up!" This isn't just a title—it's a truth. Because she showed up, I found the courage to show up too. She sparked my dreams, turned my pain into purpose, and inspired me to walk the stage and earn my Doctorate.

I am forever grateful to call her my friend, my mentor, my sister.

So raise your glass to the one, the only, turning 90 years young—Robbie Motter!

With love and gratitude,

Jennifer Blake aka JROCK 🎶 🌐 -TheLoveShark.com

Forever inspired to show up, shine bright, and lift others higher.

Let's Connect, Share & Rise Together!

Robbie Lives By A Simple Truth: Kindness Matters More Than Fame

Before launching my media and mental health ministry, Flame Alliance, I was a casting director and television producer in Hollywood for over two decades, working with countless high-profile personalities. But it's my friendship with Robbie Motter through the Global Society for Female Entrepreneurs (GSFE) that has truly transformed my journey.

Robbie lives by a simple truth: kindness matters more than fame and showing up when it's inconvenient brings the greatest rewards. She's honored me and so many others—not just with awards and recognition, but with genuine opportunities to grow, connect, and shine. Through GSFE, she's created a space where female entrepreneurs don't just network; we flourish.

What sets Robbie apart is that she's globally minded yet deeply rooted in relationships. Her influence runs deep in the hearts of everyone she meets because she shows up with authenticity, generosity, and consistent acts of service. She spreads joy and blessings without constraint.

I love Robbie deeply, and I'm honored to contribute to her legacy. She's a class act and the real deal—an inspiring mentor who walks her talk. May you live long and prosper beyond measure, my friend, and may God continue to use you for good all over the world

Roz Taylor Jordan, CEO & Founder, Flame Alliance.org
Casting Director & Producer

This Book Is A Must-Read For Anyone Seeking Inspiration To Lead And Serve Others!

My name is Liz Mejia-Celis, and I currently serve as Co-

Director of the Long Beach chapter of the Global Society
for Female Entrepreneurs (GSFE), a nonprofit organization
founded and led by CEO Robbie Motter. I have known Robbie
through my work in Glamour photography

sessions, where I collaborate with other professionals to
uplift women by helping them transform and enhance their
appearance. I have been dedicated to this work for over three
decades.

This new book that Robbie is launching is a true reflection of
her selflessness, dedication, and deep commitment to serving
others. Her story, from the very beginning, highlights her
strength,resilience, and perseverance. She embodies the ability
to overcome challenges, consistently find solutions, and lead
with authenticity. Her capacity to connect with people and
inspire them is truly exceptional.

As I read her book, I was filled with gratitude, admiration,
and honor to know her personally. I am proud to call Robbie a
mentor and role model in my life. She recognized potential in
me and encouraged me to step forward and show up, which has
opened countless opportunities. These

include leadership roles within women's groups in my region
and now the opportunity to step into the role of Director for
the Long Beach chapter.

Over the past three years as a member of the Global Society
for Female Entrepreneurs, I have had the privilege of meeting
extraordinary women and expanding my global reach. I have
traveled to London, United Kingdom, received an honorary
doctorate degree, joined the global

network Leaders Of All Nations International (LOANI),

received multiple awards, and was honored with an ambassadorship from HRM Queen Eden Soriano Trinidad, Prime Minister of Birland State. These experiences were made possible through the powerful connections Robbie creates and nurtures.

Robbie is deeply committed to helping, inspiring, and motivating women through her organization. This book is a must-read for anyone seeking inspiration to lead and serve others. Robbie leads from the heart, and her story will undoubtedly inspire others to follow in her footsteps and create meaningful impact.

Amb Dr. (h.c.) Elizabeth Mejia-Celis, Owner, Photo Styles by Liz
Award-Winning Photographer, Image Expert
Co-Director, Long Beach GSFE Network
Visit my website at www.photostylesbyliz.com
email: photostylesbyliz@gmail.com,
https://Facebook.com/liz.celisl
IG: @photostylesbyliz

To Know Robbie Is To Know What It Means to Show Up

There are some women whose lives speak long before they ever open their mouths. Their presence carries wisdom. Their footsteps leave courage in the ground behind them. Their love creates rooms where other women finally feel safe enough to stand tall. Lady Ambassador Dr. (h.c.) Robbie Motter is one of those women.

To know Robbie is to know what it means to show up, not just when life is easy, but when it is demanding, uncomfortable, uncertain, or unseen. Long before "purpose" became a buzzword and "women's empowerment" became an industry, Robbie was living it. Quietly. Faithfully. Relentlessly. This book is not simply a memoir; it is a testimony written in action, sacrifice, consistency, and love.

She Showed Up is the story of a woman who learned early what it meant to stand alone and made a lifelong decision that no other woman on her watch would ever have to do the same. From the tender vulnerability of her childhood to the unshakable confidence of her leadership today, Robbie's journey reminds us that purpose is not assigned by comfort, privilege, or applause. Purpose is forged in perseverance. It is strengthened by service. It is sustained by faith.

What makes this book extraordinary is not just what Robbie has accomplished, but how she has accomplished it. Page after page reveals a woman who did not wait to be chosen, validated, or invited. She chose herself, again and again, and then spent her life teaching other women how to do the same. She showed up in rooms where she didn't know the language. She showed up when her body was tired but her mission was still calling. She showed up for women before they knew how to show up for themselves.

This is a book for every woman who has ever questioned her worth, delayed her dream, or wondered if it was "too late." Robbie answers that question with her life: Purpose never retires. Faith never expires. Courage does not age. And impact multiplies when we refuse to sit down.

As a mentor, sister, and dear friend, I have watched Robbie lift crowns off her own head and place them gently on others while reminding women of their dignity, their power, and their divine assignment. Her leadership is not loud, but it is lasting. Not self-serving, but deeply sacrificial. Not performative, but profoundly transformational.

As you read these pages, you will not only meet Robbie, but you will meet yourself. You will hear the whisper that says, Stand up. Speak up. Show up. You will be reminded that your presence matters, your story matters, and your obedience matters.

This book is an invitation. An invitation to stop waiting. To stop shrinking. To stop doubting. And to start showing up fully, faithfully, and unapologetically.
Ambassador Dr. (h.c.) AnGèle M. Cade
CEO & Owner of Executive On the Go
GSFE Vice Chair and Board Member
Executive Pastor of Victory Bible Church of Pasadena
angelecade.com | @gelebox

Robbie Motter: A Shining Beacon of Light for Women Everywhere!

Robbie Motter is a shining beacon of light for women across the globe — truly one of the brightest stars in our galaxy.

Her "Show Up and Ask" philosophy is a living testament to her courage, tenacity, and unwavering belief that everyone deserves a seat at the table. Rooted in the aloha spirit of her Hawaiian beginnings, Robbie rose from extraordinary circumstances. Growing up in an orphanage, she met life's challenges with resilience, grace, and an unshakable inner light.

With bold dreams and an open heart, she journeyed to Los Angeles, built a powerful career, and rose to remarkable heights — even serving within the White House at one point in her journey. Every step of her path reflects determination, integrity, and a deep commitment to service.

As the founder of G.S.F.E. ~ (Global Society of Female Entrepreneurs), Robbie has created far more than an organization. She has built a global sanctuary for women — a place where business meets wisdom, insight, life lessons, and empowerment are freely shared. She has a rare gift for gathering extraordinary women, creating safe and sacred spaces where authentic connections form, and then gracefully stepping back to let the magic unfold.

To me, Robbie is a mentor, a shero, a dance partner, a party buddy, a best friend — and above all, family. This book reflects the radiant light she brings into all of our lives. Though she grew up without a traditional family, Robbie has created something even greater: one expansive, loving family of women from every corner of the world.

#WEAREFAMILY

Robbie, may you feel the love, gratitude, and deep appreciation that surrounds you. May you always know how profoundly you have touched countless lives — including mine.

With love and gratitude,

Kelly Breaux
KellyBreauxFitness@gmail.com
www.hoopitupkids.com

~~~~~~~~~~~~~~~~~~

There Are Books, Many Volumes Of Them, And Then There Is THE BOOK By ROBBIE MOTTER!

What sets them apart is that in Robbie Motter's She Showed Up! A Woman of Purpose, Power and Grace, Robbie Motter not only lives her story with amazing success, but shares it in such an incredibly inspiring way that she motivates all who read "She Showed Up!" to implement the teachings and become better for the effort - and it does require effort! However, the results are grand and last a lifetime! Powerful reading!

Love,

The Pink Lady Jackie Goldberg
Young and Showing Up at 93!
pinkladypresents.com

~~~~~~~~~~~~~~~~~~

A Tribute to the Visionary and Compassionate Spirit of Dr. Robbie Motter

Let me tell you about the extraordinary, caring, and truly inspiring Lady Ambassador Dr. Robbie Motter.

Robbie is the founder of the renowned organization, Global Society for Female Entrepreneurs (GSFE). Its mission is to empower, inspire, educate, mentor, and connect women so they can become successful entrepreneurs and lead fulfilling, abundant lives. This mission is brought to life through dynamic networking events, special excursions, training sessions, coaching, and ongoing support—all designed to help individuals realize their full potential and pursue their dreams.

Robbie's infectious enthusiasm and unwavering support, along with the dedication of her GSFE Sisters, continually motivate women, men, and youth to show up and engage. Robbie often says, "Showing up is like a treasure map—you never know what treasure you will find." Her belief in the power of community and connection opens countless doors—mentorship opportunities, training, collaborations—that help propel our dreams and grow our businesses. The possibilities are truly endless.

Robbie is a vibrant force of energy! Her remarkable insight and ability to see potential in others are truly uncanny. Many of her GSFE sisters, myself included, have been encouraged to write chapters in her books. Though some of us initially protested, myself included, Robbie's perseverance and encouragement transformed hesitation into achievement. Today, many of these women, have gone on to write their own books— a testament to her inspiring influence.

Just recently, I was browsing in my local market and came across a book about Dr. Jane Goodall, the revered primatologist. The first paragraph highlighted how few people in history embody qualities like kindness, philanthropy, grace, and goodness—names like Jane Goodall, Dr. Martin Luther King, Gandhi, and Abraham Lincoln. I believe Robbie belongs on this esteemed list. Her life's work has profoundly impacted countless lives, and her encouragement continues to inspire limitless possibilities.

As Robbie approaches her ninetieth birthday, I am confident that her upcoming book will be a tremendous success. It will be filled with nuggets of wisdom and insights from the brilliant mind of Lady Ambassador Dr. Robbie Motter. I look forward to reading it and sharing her invaluable message with the world.

Happy reading to all!

Joanne Groch
GSFE Founding Member, Educator, and Entrepreneur

~~~~~~~~~~~~~~~~~~

She Shows Up: a Woman of Purpose and Unstoppable Faith

I met Robbie Motter 30+ years ago. I can't remember exactly how we met nor do I want to remember my life before her. I love how she always steps up to support women owning their power and their gifts and talents.

At my bachelorette party we each told our God stories that we kept dear to our hearts. She told us how an angel had saved her
~~~~~~~~~~~~~~~~~~

life when she was about to be in a horrible accident. She is an example of living in faith and believing in angels, in each other and in yourself in all she does.

When Robbie called me to create a FUN Day for the Professional Women's Roundtable (PWR) National Association of Female Executives Affiliate, I was nervous and yet trusted Robbie that she knew I was the woman for the job. I got clear on the vision: Awakening us to taking care of ourselves, healing, play, learning new skills in balance, making an action plan, and creating a network of Balance Buddies while raising money for the PWR scholarship. In addition, we were to increase awareness of PWR, create new networks, partnerships and bring in new members.

For a year, she supported me in creating a team, getting an entire building at Claremont College and lots of amazing speakers, vendors and attendees.

We opened each of our conference planning meetings with a positive statement of how we envisioned the conference day. We shared a little about how our weeks were going. We planned and played, disagreed and came to agreement, stretched our abilities and felt scared. We ended each meeting holding hands, taking turns each time in saying some special closing words.

We created a great day for more than 150 women (and some men). I know that the effect of the conference has rippled, changing these women - some in small ways, some more profoundly. And it has changed us, the conference planners. We've learned not only a new model of conference planning, but a new model of how we can work hard together in joy and creativity.

It was a huge success, and we won the National NICE Award from NAFE - Network Innovation Certificate of Excellence (NICE) for this conference.

"The Day of DE Stressing, Reenergizing, and Having Fun, was the most unique and rewarding experience I have ever had. The workshops were interesting and were presented professionally. I enjoyed the "casual" nature of the entire day. We were left to decide what we wanted to do and when. My life is so hectic, I rarely get the option to "choose" where I want to be. If I wanted to sit in on a particular workshop, I could. If I wanted to leave that workshop, I could. If I wanted to shop for the tempting items that were displayed, I could. If I wanted to wander the campus aimlessly, I could... Because of the well thought out organization of this conference, by the end of the day I was able to DE Stress, Reenergized and Have Fun." Robbie Motter; Founder/Director PWR

Since that experience, I have never looked back. Her love and encouragement have helped me to support people trapped in work addiction to find harmony with their work and lives. In addition, we help to create and run programs for Military, Veterans, First Responders and their families. Thank you, Robbie, for showing me and US how to show up as our authentic selves and to find our calling and to live it out LOUD.

I love you!!!

Amy Frost, MBA, M.A. Spiritual Psychology Visiting Professor, Consultant, College of Integrative Health, DSIA & Third Responders Co-Director,

Akamal University, www.akamai.university

National Advisory Board, Adopt a Cop/Veteran/Healthcare

Worker, Wellness & Veterans Affairs Advisor, www.adopt-a-cop.org

Business, Career and Wellness Program Director (Facilitator/ Mentor/Coach), Career Institute: www.cinow.org

Flowerful Living Wellness Community Founding Member
Author, A Workaholics Guide to Resilience at Work: Life/ Work Harmony
amy@amyfrost.com email
www.facebook.com/amyfrost222 Facebook
https://www.linkedin.com/in/frostamy Linkedin
Resources For Resilience: www.energypsych.org/resilience

~~~~~~~~~~~~~~~~~~~~

Because You, Robbie... Believed in Me

When people say you meet someone at the right time and in the right place, that perfectly describes our connection. For years, I had heard about this incredible woman named Robbie, a woman of grace and a true powerhouse. I watched women transform before my eyes, gaining confidence in a remarkably short time. In my 40 years of business and networking groups, I had never seen anything like it. I was so curious... who was Robbie Motter?

When I met you unexpectedly at the North San Diego County GSFE chapter meeting, I knew instantly—it was you. Angelic and poised, a gentle soul with a powerful presence. You were kind, engaged, and truly present. You took the time
~~~~~~~~~~~~~~~~~~~~

to learn who I was and what I wanted to accomplish, and without hesitation, you began sharing your wisdom, offering encouragement and inspiration. I couldn't wait to see you again.

A few months later, I learned you were hosting a vision board event. I was flying home from across the country the night before, exhausted—but I didn't care. I had to be there. And that day, as you say, "I showed up!" From that moment on, blessings began to flow. You reignited my soul and reconnected me to what once made me successful. Through your inspiration, love, and unwavering support, I rediscovered my passion and began moving forward with excitement...no matter the challenges.

Because you truly saw something in me, and in what I wanted to achieve, whether through your direct encouragement, your recommendations, or the extraordinary community of powerhouse women you opened the door to, my life changed. You helped me see the power within myself. And while I had to "Show up and Ask," it was your belief, influence, and guidance that made those opportunities possible.

Through the incredible community of women entrepreneurs and leaders I met because of you, I became a co-author in two #1 International Best Seller books, an Ambassador of LOANI, received my Humanitarian Doctorate from Global International Alliance, and was honored with nominations and awards recognizing leadership and service. Most importantly, I am finally owning the God-given talents entrusted to me. After five years in the making, I have now launched my nonprofit, A Happy Hero Foundation.

Thank you for reminding me to believe in myself, to keep showing up even when I don't feel like it, and to ASK.

Your belief didn't just change my path—it awakened my purpose.

With great love and gratitude,

Lady Dr. (h.c.) Amb. Nanette Meneses

~~~~~~~~~~~~~~~~~

The Robbie Motter Effect -The Power of Showing Up

Each day represents a new beginning, a fresh start to engage with people we know as well as meet new people along the way. What is indeed special is when we meet that special person who seeks to find ways to inspire us to go beyond what we know, to learn more about the world we live in and in turn, ourselves. The day that changed my life is the day that I met Ms. Robbie Motter.

I'd like to share with you a special, life changing moment that took place with Robbie Motter. In August 2024, I experienced a moment that quietly and profoundly reshaped my understanding of service, global connection, and personal fulfillment. What began as an early-morning Zoom meeting with GSFE became a life changing moment for me that opened my eyes to see the world from a refreshing global perspective.

Like many virtual meetings, the morning began with a brief technical delay. I experienced a small Zoom issue while logging in. Once resolved, I was present among my fellow GSFE members with the United States flag behind us representing our nation. The screen with humanitarian
~~~~~~~~~~~~~~~~~

leaders with their respective flags displayed on their screens
— participants from China, Japan, the United Kingdom,
Canada, Australia, Europe and other regions of the world—
each sharing their commitment to making a positive difference
in the world. In that moment, it was clear that being present
with Robbie Motter on that day truly mattered.

As the meeting commenced, I was nurtured by the atmosphere
of positivity and the human connection. Hundreds of
participants filled the screen, each sharing their own story,
mission, and vision. It was a powerful illustration of what can
happen when people come together with purpose.

Throughout the meeting, participants shared insights into
their humanitarian work. Each story reflected a commitment
to service through education, community development, health
initiatives, or support for vulnerable populations. As each
person shared their story, it was clear that we all shared the
common purpose of serving communities through passionate
outreach.

When Robbie Motter shared her story with the global group
of participants, her message was truly heartfelt. She expressed
sincere gratitude to everyone for showing up. Her remarks
were thoughtful, heartfelt, and inclusive. In that moment,
I recognized that GSFE is more than an organization; it is
a global community built on shared values and respect for
authentic human connection. It was a reminder that peace
and progress begin with intentional actions—showing
up, listening, and working together. That message became
especially clear during that special Zoom. We all felt a sense
of joy through meeting new people as we shared moments of
mutual recognitions and heartfelt connection.

Since that August meeting, I have found myself more motivated to think and engage from a broader global perspective. GSFE has reinforced my belief that through working together, we can establish meaningful connections and lasting impact within our nation and around the world. The experience encouraged me to dream bigger, to ask more of myself, and to approach service with renewed clarity and commitment.

That morning was more than a virtual meeting; it was a trajectory of what is possible when people choose unity over division and purpose over convenience. I am grateful to Robbie Motter for her belief in all of us as members of GSFE. Her inner strength, intellectual brilliance, and elegance are an inspiration to us all. I am inspired by her each day to continue to cultivate a space where collaboration, recognition, and shared humanity are prioritized. Together we have the power to create opportunities to connect with others in ways that expand our perspective and deepen our understanding of our purpose as human beings.

As I think about it now, I understand that meaningful growth often occurs when we step beyond our comfort zones...and take a step forward to show up and participate with others and step out to engage on each new day with courage and hope. Showing up is an exercise of connecting with others that you know and new people you are going to meet along the way. Our connection together is the authentic key to success and happiness. I learn this from Robbie Motter each day.

Belinda Foster, GSFE Publicist
Email: awjplatinumpr@gmail.com

Robbie Motter Has Many Lessons to Offer

Robbie Motter has so many lessons to offer to so many people; two, in particular, stand out for me.

In 1989, I heard about an all-night high school graduation "lock-in" party designed to keep graduates safe while they celebrated. I asked my daughter if any of her friends' parents might help. Her best friend's mother, Robbie, showed up to the planning meeting—an act that led to what became a hugely successful, first-ever graduation party.

Years earlier, when Robbie was just 15, her boss told her that as a woman she would have to succeed entirely on her own, as there was no time to help her. Robbie made a vow that day: she would always make time to help others, especially women. For more than 70 years, she has honored that promise. She transformed a painful experience into the powerful practice of "showing up" for countless women—a practice I have followed for most of my own life.

Our friendship grew over the years, and I have watched Robbie teach, lead, and create remarkable opportunities for hundreds simply by showing up—and by teaching others to do the same. She has continued to show up for me, time and again, and her example has shaped many lives in lasting ways.

Gillian Larson. Public speaker

Tribute to Lady Ambassador Dr. Robbie Motter

I celebrate the wonderful new book about the life of an extraordinary individual who has profoundly impacted my life and the lives of many others—Lady Ambassador Robbie Motter. Our friendship began when I served at the San Jacinto Chamber of Commerce, where Robbie's unwavering support and guidance became instrumental in shaping my journey as a leader.

As the CEO and Founder of the Global Society for Female Entrepreneurs, a remarkable non-profit organization, Robbie has dedicated herself to creating a better world through innovative ideas and tireless efforts. Her ability to think outside the box has led to numerous fundraising initiatives, making it possible for our Oceanside Chapter to thrive and serve those in need.

Robbie's commitment to empowering others is evident in her decision to appoint me as the Director of our chapter. This opportunity not only allowed me to grow as a leader but also to collaborate with diverse individuals who share a passion for making a difference. Her vision and enthusiasm inspire those around her to reach new heights, and I am truly grateful for the chance to contribute to our mission under her guidance.

What sets Robbie apart is her genuine kindness and unwavering dedication to uplift others. She approaches every challenge with positivity and determination, fostering an environment where creativity and collaboration flourish. It is an honor to call her my friend and mentor.

As we continue to work together to create impactful change in our community, let us all take a moment to appreciate Robbie's invaluable contributions. May her passion inspire us to push boundaries and pursue excellence in all our endeavors.

Thank you, Robbie, for everything you do. Your legacy is one of hope, leadership, and unwavering commitment to helping others.

With heartfelt gratitude,
Ambassador Dr. (h.c.) Cheri Reynolds
Co-Director, GSFE Oceanside Network

~~~~~~~~~~~~~~~~~~~

I have been blessed to have had an opportunity to meet and know Lady Amb. Dr. Robbie Motter through GSFE and LOANI. The most profound moments have been to listen to her wisdom of ages through motivational and Inspirational talks in events and conferences. What inspires me most is her power and ability to invite her audience to her world through her Mottos and Mantra's. "It's All About Showing Up and Asking;- We don't Compete but Complete each other". Her presence resonates with the powerful energy and the warmth she possesses as she "Walks the Talk".

With great affection, Lady Robbie Motter has planted and watered valuable seeds in my life to always give of ourselves to service without reservation. Being an author in one of her best seller books "What's your Why" gave me an opportunity to open up my wounded self from domestic abuse to a healing journey. She made me feel a victor that I not only survived but overcame becoming the Unstoppable Beautiful Soul, that l am.
~~~~~~~~~~~~~~~~~~~

These values of opening up, sharing and resilience have enabled me to share my world with others who may be struggling with diverse personality issues. At 90, She is still smart, purposed, focused, resilient, and ever showing up, she has challenged me to build confidence to unlock and achieve my full potential. She has motivated me not to shy from asking where I may not understand. I have acquired a renewed knowledge that we all possess unlimited possibilities to impact one another no matter what stage we are in life. Her warmth and sparkling grandiose provokes my faith to focus on the possibilities that life offers for change. I have since become a "Global Change Maker" changing the world to be a better place to live in. Lady Robbie enjoys not only celebrating her own legacy but also putting it in her publication works for future generations to come.

Eminent Peace Ambassador Dr (h.c) Winfred Wanjiku Gitonga.

I've Known Robbie 20 Years And Never Met Anyone Else Like Her

Robbie gives new meaning to what it truly means to live your life—to show up fully, to be present, and to be a light, regardless of what life has placed in your path.

She has a pure heart; unlike any I have ever seen. It's the kind of heart that feels rare in this world—one rooted in deep compassion, grace, and unwavering love for others.

Robbie also has a gift.

A remarkable one.

She sees things in people that they often cannot see in themselves.

She calls forth purpose, strength, and possibility simply by believing in others so deeply.

But what makes Robbie truly extraordinary is this: she doesn't just show up to events, stages, or moments to share her voice or shine her light.

She shows up in people's lives.

She shows up authentically. Beautifully. Consistently.

Robbie hasn't just lived a life of significance—she has shown countless others how to live one too. Through her actions, her presence, and her unwavering faith in God and humanity, she teaches by example what it means to love boldly and lead with heart.

In her book, Robbie not only shares the struggles she has faced in her own life, but she shows us something far more powerful: that life is not about what happens to us—it's about how we respond.

Because every single person will experience difficulty and suffering. That is part of being human.

What Robbie shows us, through this beautiful book she has written, is that when we practice gratitude, when we offer unconditional love to others, and when we uplift one another—across race, background, and circumstance—life can not only be beautiful, but we will also meet truly beautiful people along the way.

I treasure my friendship with Robbie. I treasure and thank God every day for placing her in my life.

And I encourage you to grab a copy of this book. It will change your life. It will change how you think about life. And most importantly, I believe it will help you move forward—and strive to live and love a little more like Robbie.

Because we need more beautiful souls like Robbie in the world!

Amb. Lauren Raguzin

~~~~~~~~~~~~~~~~

A Woman of Purpose, Power and Unstoppable Faith

My spouse, Joseph, and I were invited to a party hosted by one of his clients. He has a very high-level clientele, and many of them would be at the party. And, while Joseph is well-known to all of them, I knew I would know none of them.

Normally, as a successful author and businesswoman, I would be fine with being a newbie. However, due to a health issue, I haven't felt like my usual self, lacking both energy and confidence. So, even though I knew Joseph really wanted to go to the party and wouldn't go without me, I was searching for a good excuse not to .

Then I read Robbie's words: "I showed up when I was tired, hurting, overwhelmed, unsure, or walking into a room where I didn't know a single soul." And she reminded me that "showing up is the hinge that swings open every door." So I pulled myself together and agreed to join Joseph.
~~~~~~~~~~~~~~~~

As it turned out, I was glad I showed up to the party. People were happy to meet me. I was glad to meet them. They shared experiences, took pictures and texted them to me, and we had more than a few good laughs. There was no moment when I regretted being there. In fact, as I rode home that night, I was thinking about the people I met and how interesting everyone was; I was glad I went.

So If you ever feel like sitting out the next networking event or needing a gentle kick in the butt to get going, open this book – to any page – and read a paragraph or two. Robbie's right about the importance of showing up. Digest the wisdom she shares and you'll get the power you need to move forward.

Happy 90th birthday, Robbie, and best wishes for a fabulously victorious year ahead!

Annmarie Kelly, Author/Speaker
Founder, The Victorious Woman Project

~~~~~~~~~~~~~~~~~~

She's A Wonderful Role Model!

I am so honored and grateful to be asked to give not only my mentor, but my friend Ambassador Dr. Lady Robbie Motter a testimony of how amazing she is not only as a leader of GSFE, but a spokesperson for female entrepreneurs.

I walked into a GSFE meeting in South Orange County many years ago as a guest of Shellie Hunt, not knowing anything about the group, and ended up sitting next to this lady who is
~~~~~~~~~~~~~~~~~~

completely dolled up head to toe and just fabulous.

We got to talking and she asked me if I had a book and I said, "Why, yes, I do!" She said, "I would like to buy it," which she did.   Little did I know I'd be getting all these awards now for Author of the Year, Best Author. Getting speaking offers at all the GSFE locations and one thing led to another.

I have since had a complete wall full of award certificates, just by meeting this extraordinary woman.

She is there to help everyone and support all these women in their journey by yes telling them to show up and ask for what they want which has been her secret and her bottom line to success.

I look up to this woman! I adore this woman and appreciate everything she does not only for me, but for all the ladies that she comes into contact with.   She has just been a wonderful role model and anytime I don't feel like driving somewhere I think of her driving all over to attend meetings without hesitation.

Robbie you are amazing and just fabulous. Love you with all my heart!

Ambassador Dr. Lauren M. Powers

~~~~~~~~~~~~~~~~~~~~~~

Robbie Motter Changed My Life By How She Showed Up In It

She loved me without judgment. She saw me at my worst—my
~~~~~~~~~~~~~~~~~~~~~~

chaos, my noise, my unraveling—and she never flinched. When I couldn't see past the wreckage, she saw the woman beneath it. When I disappeared into survival mode, she gently kept inviting me back. Not pushing—just standing there, steady, saying with her presence: I still believe you belong here.

That's when it hit me: Robbie is a champion for all women—especially the ones who feel too broken, too loud, too messy, or "too much" to deserve unconditional support. She fights for healing women, overlooked women, underestimated women. The ones still pretending they have it together. The ones who truly do. She champions them all.

Even now, in her later years, Robbie is unstoppable. A force to be reckoned with. A woman who doesn't fade—she amplifies. She has power without apology, love without condition, and impact without needing the spotlight. And yet, anyone who crosses her path feels the brilliance of her mission.

She was instrumental to my nonprofit, and even more instrumental to me. Not because she fixed me—but because she refused to define me by what was breaking me. She helped me reconnect to my purpose, my worth, and eventually, my healing.

Robbie doesn't just support women—she defends their becoming.

Her legacy isn't loud speeches or grand announcements. It's lives quietly rewritten. Mine is one of them. And I will always be grateful that my story intersected with hers.

Dawn Schultz

You embody all the qualities of a best friend, mother, and mentor.

Your wisdom is more than just professional guidance; it's advice that I and many others across continents are eager to embrace. It is because of your example, transparency, and authenticity.

Whether your advice is shared within the pages of your books, spoken from behind your desk, or offered through a teary-eyed listening session, you are always heard and deeply appreciated. Whenever I open and read your weekly "Positive Message" to the GSFE & LOANI Sisters, Brothers, and friends, I hear it in your loving voice. It feels as though you are speaking directly to me.

I am so glad you have authored so many books, Robbie. This means that long after my love for you has faded, your wisdom and love will continue to touch many for generations to come.

With all my love,

Stone Love Fauré
Former GSFE Northern California Director

Author | Speaker | Retreat Leader | Certified Pilates Instructor

Dr (h.c.)Stone Love Fauré is the premier award winning international speaker, writer and mentor for women entrepreneurs and the go-to expert for Decision-Making. She is the recipient of the Presidential Award and an Honorary Doctorate in Humanities Award. Dr Stone is an international retreat leader and certified coach with over 20 years of coaching experience.

She is the author of 3 Best Selling Books
WWW.DECISIONTIMESTONELOVE.COM

Stoneologys: "Solid Wisdom That Brings Out The Brilliance In You

~~~~~~~~~~~~~~~~

"Faith Woven into Fashion"

Before joining the Global Society for Female Entrepreneurs (GSFE), I was already a designer with talent, vision, and creativity, but GSFE helped me see myself differently.

Through GSFE, I learned the true power of showing up. Not just physically, but confidently. Fully. Authentically.

I learned to believe in myself more deeply, to ask without fear, and to trust that my voice and my story mattered.

GSFE encouraged and inspired me to participate in multiple collaborative book chapters, and through that experience, something powerful was awakened in me. Those opportunities gave me the courage to write and publish my own anthology, "What Are You Wearing?" The Inspirational and Spiritual Side of Fashion. That book became a reflection of my purpose: using fashion as a platform for faith, inspiration, and self-expression.

Because of GSFE, I began stepping into greater visibility and opportunity. I am now doing more fashion shows, expanding my reach as a celebrity designer, and confidently walking in rooms I once only dreamed of entering.
~~~~~~~~~~~~~~~~

Through GSFE's global connections, Leaders of all Nations (Loani) and Global International Alliance (GIA) I traveled to England, where I received an Honorary Humanitarian Doctorate Degree as well as an award in parliament - an experience that forever changed how I see my work and my calling.

GSFE also opened the door for meaningful collaboration.

Through my company, Ochea Fashions, I formed a powerful partnership to support Ulang a nonprofit that supports widows and orphans in Sudan doing humanitarian work , allowing my designs to serve a purpose far beyond the runway.

As a result of GSFE and the work I continue to do in service and leadership, I have received numerous honors and awards, including Presidential Awards.

Each recognition reminds me that when purpose meets courage, lives are touched.

GSFE didn't just support my business, it helped me step into my purpose. It reminded me that I am worthy of being seen, heard, and celebrated.

Most importantly, it taught me that when women support women, incredible things happen.

I showed up.
I asked.
I believed.
And my life expanded in ways I never imagined.
Ambassador Dr. Chebra Dorsey
Celebrity Designer | #1 US and International best-selling author

Humanitarian
Founder, Ochea Fashions
Ocheafashion1@gmail.com, Facebook, Chebra Dorsey or ocheafashionproduction or ocheafashionboutique and Instagram Ocheafashion

---

"Finding My Voice Again: From Retirement to Purpose Through GSFE"

Before joining GSFE, I believed I had reached the stage of retirement and that my most active years were behind me. I never imagined there was still so much more inside me to give. GSFE helped me rediscover purpose, confidence, and passion I didn't even realize I still carried.

Soon after joining, I produced several sold-out Christmas dinner shows in our community. What began as a small step of courage grew into something much bigger. I went on to co-produce special annual events featuring more than ten performers at each show. I also served as the sound producer for emcees and dancers, helping create joyful, professional, and memorable experiences for everyone involved.

I have always loved to write, but I never believed publication was something possible for me. Through GSFE, that belief changed. I am now a published author in four collaborative books—something I once only dreamed about. GSFE opened doors I never knew existed.

That ripple of opportunity extended to my family as well. My sister, Lisette Fournier in Quebec, Canada, entered a poetry contest organized by Queen Eden. Her poem was selected and published in a book that now resides in the oldest library in the world. What an incredible thrill and honor that was for her—and for all of us.

In 2020, my life took a frightening turn when I contracted COVID and spent three weeks in intensive care. When I finally returned home on oxygen, weak and recovering, GSFE surrounded me with love. They prayed for me, supported me, and even brought meals to help me regain my strength. That kind of compassion is something I will forever be grateful for.

GSFE has also supported my weekly karaoke shows, where many people sang publicly for the very first time. Watching them step into their courage, find their voices, and blossom brought me immense joy. Together, we grew—not just as performers, but as human beings.

Through it all, GSFE became more than a network. We became a family—one that believes in lifting each other, showing up, and reminding one another that it's never too late to dream again.

Ambassador Nicole Farrell

Nicole Farrell123@hotmail.com, http://www.frenchnote.com

A Tribute to Lady Ambassador Dr. (h.c.) Robbie Motter of GSFE: A True Partner and Esteemed Alumna of the GIA Global International Alliance Program

Lady Ambassador Robbie Motter is a remarkable woman whose life reflects unwavering service, compassion, and global impact. She has dedicated decades of her life to giving back to others across the world, embracing people of every nationality with genuine love and respect. She is a woman who gives her all to everyone she encounters, without hesitation or condition.

She is a true pillar and fearless advocate for human rights, women's rights, and the dignity of all people. Whenever there is a need, she stands firm—defending, supporting, and uplifting those who require a voice. Lady Ambassador Motter is a 24/7 servant-leader, always present in times of need, never turning away, and consistently going above and beyond to help others. She does not know the word "no" when it comes to responsibility, service, and standing for what is right.

I proudly salute her for the many years of steadfast support she has given to Global International Alliance (GIA). Her loyalty, partnership, and dedication have been a blessing to our organization and to countless lives she has touched.

As we look forward to honoring her upcoming 90th birthday in 2026, we celebrate not only her longevity but her legacy. To us, she is truly a queen—a woman who stands with all people, for all people.

May God continue to bless her life with strength, favor, peace, and abundance. Her impact is immeasurable, and her legacy will forever shine.

Lady Ambassador Dr. Lenora Peterson, Ph.D., Goodwill Ambassador

Chief Executive, Global International Alliance (GIA) - People's Choice Program

We Are One!

WE ARE ONE
WE DON'T COMPLETE
WE COMPLETE EACH OTHER
GSFE
WE ARE OF
WE DON'T COMPL
WE COMPLET EACH
GSFE

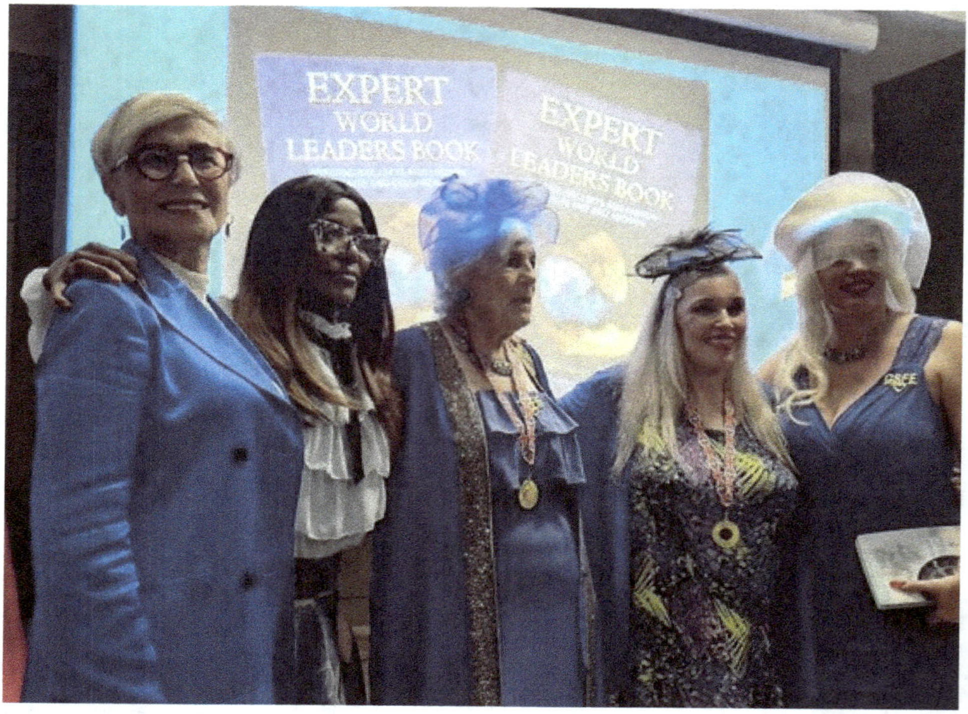

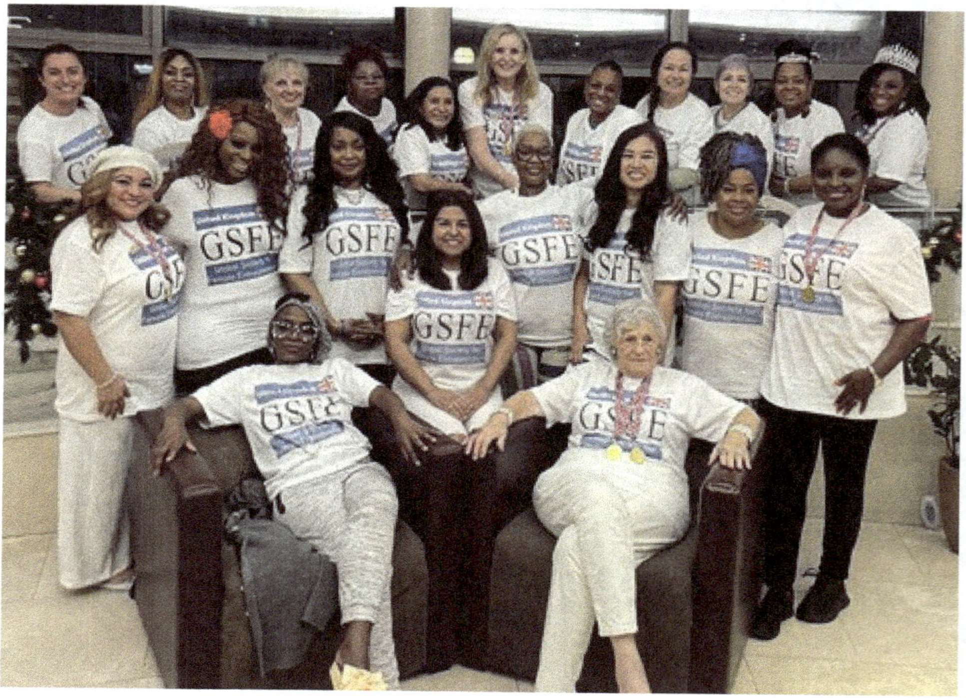

Closing Note

Thank you for sharing this journey with me.
If my story reminds you of anything, let it remind you of this:

You are stronger than you think.
Your purpose matters.
Your presence matters.
And your life can touch more people than you will ever know.

Keep showing up.
Keep believing.
Keep shining your light.

The world needs YOU.

With love,

Queen Lady Amb. Dr. (h.c.) Robbie Motter